STORIES FROM A LIFE IN SCIENCE

VOLUME X: UNKNOWNS

by

Arlan E. S. Smith, Ph.D.

Copyright © 2005 by Arlan E.S. Smith

All rights reserved. No part of this book shall be reproduced or transmitted in any form or by any means, electronic, mechanical, magnetic, photographic including photocopying, recording or by any information storage and retrieval system, without prior written permission of the publisher. No patent liability is assumed with respect to the use of the information contained herein. Although every precaution has been taken in the preparation of this book, the publisher and author assume no responsibility for errors or omissions. Neither is any liability assumed for damages resulting from the use of the information contained herein.

ISBN 0-7414-2829-6

Published by:

INFINITY
PUBLISHING.COM

1094 New DeHaven Street, Suite 100
West Conshohocken, PA 19428-2713
Info@buybooksontheweb.com
www.buybooksontheweb.com
Toll-free (877) BUY BOOK
Local Phone (610) 941-9999
Fax (610) 941-9959

Printed in the United States of America

Printed on Recycled Paper

Published October 2005

TABLE OF CONTENTS

STORIES FROM A LIFE WITH SCIENCE
VOLUME X: UNKNOWNS

CHAPTER 1
THE PURPOSE OF LIFE

THE PURPOSE OF LIFE	1
WHAT IS THE PURPOSE OF LIFE?	2
DNA FOR THE RETENTION AND TRANSFER OF INFORMATION	3
THE APPEARANCE OF NUCLEOTIDES	4
PROTEINS WOULD BE ESSENTIAL	5
COMPONENTS NEEDED FOR PROTEIN SYNTHESIS	7
THE FIRST DNA POLYMER	8
SYNTHESIS OF DNA AND "MESSENGER" RNA	9
THE IMPORTANCE OF CYCLIC TEMPERATURE	10
FROM MESSENGER TO PROTEIN WITHOUT RIBOSOMES	10
THE FIRST PROTEIN: DNA POLYMERASE?	12
THE ENHANCEMENT OF RNA AND PROTEIN SYNTHESIS	12
THE SYNTHESIS OF MEMBRANE CONSTITUENTS	13
THE IMPORTANCE OF RIBOSOMES	14
THE FORMATION OF MICELLES	15
THE IMPORTANCE OF MICELLES	16
THE INITIATION OF CELL DIVISION	16
CHANGES IN DNA BRING ADVANTAGEOUS DEVELOPMENTS	18
DEVELOPMENT OF A PHOTOSYNTHETIC SYSTEM	19
DNA: THE ULTIMATE SOLUTION TO LIFE'S PROBLEMS	20
LIFE IN COMPLEX SOCIETIES	21
HOUSING	23

TRANSPORTATION	23
COMMUNICATION	24
MEDIA	25
EDUCATION	27
INSTRUMENTS OF WAR	30
CONCLUSION	32

CHAPTER 2
THE GODS OF HUMANS ARE HUMANS

YOUTHFUL PICTURES OF GOD	33
WHERE IS HEAVEN AND WHO IS GOD?	35
A GLIMPSE INTO THE WORLDS RELIGIONS	36
BUDDHISM	36
JUDAISM	37
ISLAM	38
DHARMA	39
YOGA	39
TRANSCENDENTAL MEDITATION	40
A CHERISHED HUMAN CONCEPT	42
THE NATURE OF THE GODS OF HUMANS	43
DID A GOD CREATE THE UNIVERSE?	45
TRACKING HUMAN ORIGINS	48
THE FIRST SIGNS OF SPIRITUAL THOUGHT	54
GOD AS THE COLLECTIVE THOUGHTS OF HUMANS	55
EPILOGUE	57

CHAPTER 3
LIFE AFTER DEATH

DOES LIFE CONTINUE AFTER DEATH?	60
LIFE AFTER DEATH CONTINUES IN SPIRITUAL FORM?	62
LIFE AFTER DEATH: A POWERFUL THOUGHT	63
THE FORM OF THE HUMAN SPIRIT	65
RELIGIONS EXPOUND THE HUMANISTIC APPROACH	66

HUMAN SPIRITS PICTURED WITH HUMAN SHAPE 68
THE POWER OF THE BRAIN 69
THE BRAIN, THE MIND, AND THE SPIRIT 70
THE HUMAN BRAIN SUPERCEDES THE SPIRIT 71
SUMMARY 73

CHAPTER 4
ELIMINATING TERRORISM

HUMAN BOMBS 75
UNDERSTANDING HUMAN BOMBS 75
THE PEOPLE OF INFLUENCE 77
STRONG CONVICTIONS 78
A PARADOX: TIME AND THOUGHT AND DEATH 79
PEOPLE OF INFLUENCE
AND THE DEATH OF HUMAN BOMBS 80
THE RIGHTS OF HUMAN BOMBS AND
PEOPLE OF INFLUENCE 81
HOW TO ELIMINATE HUMAN BOMBS:
IT SEEMED SIMPLE AT FIRST 82
WHAT ABOUT THE OPPOSITION? 84
HUMANS HAVE REVERSED
THE ROLES OF GODS AND HUMANS 84
CORRECTIONS ARE IN ORDER 86
THE WORLD OF HUMAN THOUGHT 87
HUMANS MADE THEIR GODS
IN THE IMAGE OF HUMANS 88
THE POWER OF HUMAN THOUGHT 88
CHERISH THE WORLD OF HUMAN THOUGHT 89

CHAPTER 5
WOMEN SHOULD HAVE CONTROL OF THEIR OVA

EVERY OVUM HAS THE POTENTIAL FOR LIFE 90
THE FATE OF UNFERTILIZED OVA 90
QUESTIONS THAT ONLY WOMEN SHOULD ANSWER 91
PREGNANCY IS THE RULE FOR NONHUMAN PRIMATES 93

THE MENSTRUAL CYCLE GAVE WOMEN CONTROL 94
ETHICS AND MORALITY COME TO WOMEN'S OVA 95
OVA, ETHICS, MORALITY, AND ABORTION 95
RETURN THE RIGHT OF CHOICE TO THE WOMEN 96
A BETTER TECHNIQUE THAT AVOIDS ISSUES 97
WOMEN SHOULD DETERMINE THE DESTINY
OF THEIR OVA 98
THE MORALITY OF OVA AND STEM CELLS 99
THE HUMANITY AND WISDOM OF WOMEN 99

CHAPTER 6
DIVERSITY

INTRODUCTION 100
ANCIENT GREECE AND ROME 100
GENETIC DIVERSITY AND
THE DECLINE OF CIVILIZATIONS 103
ANCIENT EGYPTIANS AND GENETIC DIVERSITY 104
MESOPOTAMIA AND THE MIDDLE EAST 105
A DIFFERENCE IN THE ANCIENT MESOAMERICANS ... 105
MESOAMERICA AND THE SPANISH CONQUERERS 107
EUROPEAN RENAISSANCE 109
THE MOST DIVERSE? THE UNITED STATES 110
ATMOSPHERIC DIVERSITY 111
CONCLUSIONS 112

CHAPTER 7
HIGHLY PIGMENTED SKIN IS AN ENVIRONMENTAL ADAPTATION TO SHADE AND SHADOWS

MELANOCYTES, MELANIN AND SUN LIGHT 113
THE PRIMARY FUNCTION OF
MELANIN IS NOT PROTECTIVE 114
IN AFRICA DARK SKIN AND HAIR
ARE ADAPTATIONS FOR BLENDING WITH SHADOWS 115

IN THE NORTHERN HEMISPHERE
SKIN PIGMENT CHANGES WITH THE SEASONS 116
CHANGES IN SKIN PIGMENT FOLLOW THE SUN CYCLE ... 117
SKIN PIGMENT SERVES AS CAMOUFLAGE IN SHADE ... 117

CHAPTER 8
PHEROMONIC THEORY: INDIVIDUALITY, SEXUALITY, AND LOVE

INTRODUCTION 119
SPECIES IDENTITY... 120
ANCESTRAL AND TERRITORIAL IDENTITY......................... 121
PHEROMONES AND HETEROSEXUAL IDENTITY 121
PHEROMONES AND HOMOSEXUAL IDENTITY 123
PHEROMONES AND BISEXUAL IDENTITY 124
PHEROMONES AND LOVE... 124
PHEROMONES AND INCEST.. 127
TRUST YOUR PHEROMONES 129

CHAPTER 9
HOW I STOPPED SMOKING

DUPED BY CIGARETTE COMPANIES AND SOCIETY 131
RECOGNOZING THE SYMPTOMS: TIME TO STOP.............. 131
SWITCHING FROM CIGARETTES TO A FILTERED PIPE 132
THE FILTERS TURNED DARK BROWN................................. 133
BRAINWASHED BY ADVERTISING AND MOVIES 133
IT WAS TIME TO STOP... 134
THE EASIEST WAY TO STOP? NEVER START 134

CHAPTER 10
THE IMPORTANCE OF IODINE

DISCOVERING THE VALUE OF IODINE 135
IODINE AND HERPES SIMPLEX.. 137

PIGMENTED AREAS AND "LIVER SPOTS"	139
IODINE, AN ITCHY RASH, AND JELLY FISH	139
A MISPLACED REGENERATING NERVE	142
SMALL AREAS OF ABNORMAL EPITHELIAL GROWTH	144
IODINE ACTS ON ABNORMAL CELLS	146

CHAPTER 11
A FORMULA FOR GETTING A^S IN CLASSES

THE SIGNIFICANCE OF MAGICAL NUMBERS	148
THE 45 HOUR SCHOOL WEEK	149
THE IDEAL CLASS SCHEDULE	150
WRITTEN LISTS OF KEY WORDS	150
USING THE LISTS	151
LISTS FROM READING MATERIAL	152
LISTS FORM THE BASIS OF MY STUDY SCHEME	153
THE BRAIN THRIVES ON CHANGE AND NEW INFORMATION	155
GRADUATE SCHOOL WAS VERY DIFFERENT	156
MOTIVATION FOR GRADUATE SCHOOL	156
I BECAME A STUDENT AGAIN	157
TESTING THE POWER OF MY BRAIN	157
MY STUDY SCHEME WORKED WELL	159
I MADE THE PRESIDENT'S SCHOLARS LIST	159

PREFACE

This is "Volume X" in an eight volume series. entitled STORIES FROM A LIFE IN SCIENCE by Arlan E. S. Smith, Ph.D. The X in Volume X does not represent roman numeral ten but the X in math and science, the unknown. This is the seventh volume in the series and is the volume in which I bring together miscellaneous thoughts and theories that I have had over the years. It deals with a few controversial topics to which I bring solutions. It also covers several items that have helped me maintain a healthy life. Most of the chapters are unrelated but they present solutions to problems that should be shared with other humans throughout the world.

Chapter 1

THE PURPOSE OF LIFE

In informal conversations, formal discussions, and on certain types of television programs I have encountered attempts to bring meaning to the question, "what is the meaning of life"? I too, have given this question considerable thought, and have come to the conclusion that the question has no meaning. "What is the meaning of life" can have numerous answers. In reality, the answers can be as numerous as the human population. Each individual could develop a personal meaning of life that would only apply to that individual, or a collection of individuals could focus on a meaning that applied to the collection, such as the gathering of millions of catholics in Rome for the burial of Pope John Paul II and the inauguration of Pope Benedict XVI. They might be seeking a uniformity of belief that would bring the collection to the "meaning of life". How many collections of individuals, who seek uniformity of belief, might there be in this world? There must be at least thousands, if not hundreds of thousands of collections seeking uniform beliefs. The reason for so many collections? Each collection seeks, perhaps, slightly different beliefs, hence, will bring a different meaning to the "meaning of life". If they didn't bring a different meaning, there would only be a few collections, or only one collection of totally uniform beliefs. Then the question would be insubordinately valid. However, that is not the world wide case. There are many collections of people, each brings their own interpretation to the question. In the end, the question "what is the meaning of life" has numerous answers and perhaps billions of interpretations. This invalidates the question and renders it meaningless. A question with such numerous answers, means that that question has any answer that anyone would wish to give. This is not the kind of question I am interested in answering. To the question: "What is the meaning of life?" I could give any meaning that I wished.

WHAT IS THE PURPOSE OF LIFE?

I am interested in answering a question that solves the great mystery of life as it has existed for billions of years on our planet, Earth. A question that has been of interest to humans since the appearance of beautiful paintings on the walls of the caves in France and Spain. The hominids on Earth have been seeking an answer to that all important question long before they developed a written language, so, the question please. WHAT IS THE PURPOSE OF LIFE? That is the question, and I mean the "purpose of life", not the meaning of life. These are two very different things, the purpose of life as it has existed on Earth since before the beginning of life should have one and only one answer. The meaning of life only has value to beings who can understand meaning, so that limits the question and the answer to only one form of life, namely, humans. While, "the purpose of life", and the answer to the purpose extend far beyond one species to include all species, and the development of life even before living cells came into existence.

The answer to the question of purpose is far more important than the question itself. All of life on Earth has experienced or sought the single answer to the "purpose of life" since the infliction of life on the surface of the Earth. Humans, modern men and women in particular, have looked for an answer to the question of purpose and we still seek an answer to this all important question.

Do I have an answer to the question? Yes!

The purpose of life is TO SOLVE PROBLEMS.

This applies to all life in the present and to all life in the past. Extinct species were no longer able to solve their problems, so they went extinct. All living species have been able to solve their problems, so they are living in the world today. That includes humans and their hominid ancestors that go back in history to at least six million years ago to *Orrorin tugenensis*.

This is taking a huge step foreword, I would like to go back in time to a period before cells came into existence, to a time when the essentials for the chemistry of life were under development. These were the problems that had to be solved before life could begin.

DNA FOR THE RETENTION AND TRANSFER OF INFORMATION

The very first problem that needed a solution began before life came into existence. Life needed a form that could sustain and perpetuate the attributes of life from one moment to the next, from one year to the ensuing year, from one millennium to the next. To find the form that solved this problem, we only have to turn to life as it exists in the present. The universal form that sustains and perpetuates life giving attributes is found in living organisms from the mightiest bacteria to the greatest human. All cells possess giant molecules of deoxyribonucleic acid, DNA. These molecules are the hereditarily active components of all cells and consist of a phosphate group bound to a deoxyribose sugar which can be bound to one of four nucleotide bases, adenine, thymine, guanine, or cytosine. In a large DNA molecule the sugars are bonded one to the other through phosphate groups with a nucleotide base bonded to each sugar along the phosphate linked polymer of deoxyribose sugars. When a single stranded DNA polymer is duplicated, the nucleotide adenine always hydrogen bonds to thymine or the nucleotide thymine always pairs with adenine on the polymer, and the nucleotide guanine always hydrogen bonds with cytosine or the nucleotide cytosine always pairs with guanine on the polymer. This pairing is very strict because that is the only way that they can form hydrogen bonds, but it assures exact duplication from one DNA polymer to the next. The order of the four bases along the polymer might appear to be random, and it probably was random at first, but eventually they appeared in orders of three, because each triplet of nucleotide bases eventually became the code for an amino acid. This gives DNA the important property of storing the information that is required for the perpetuation of life. Eventually the system of complement duplication with chemically paired nucleotides would provide the basis for the retention and transfer of information from one DNA molecule to the next. This would enable the perpetuation of information essential for life and sustain that information as it came into being many millions of millenia ago. Thus, the development of DNA molecules solved the first problem that would enable the development of life on Earth, and set the course for the purpose of life.

THE APPEARANCE OF NUCLEOTIDES

From the above discourse, we obviously have another problem that needed a solution. What was the origin of the nucleotides that were needed for the synthesis of DNA? Following the experiments of Stanly Miller and Harold Urey, it has been shown that an electrical discharge passing through a gaseous mixture of formaldehyde and hydrogen cyanide would result in the formation of nucleotide bases and ribose sugars, so there seems to be no difficulty in obtaining the synthesis of nucleotides in an atmosphere charged with carbon compounds of various types. Lightning bolts were supposedly very prevalent in the early atmosphere of Earth. Lightning could readily supply greater quantities of the same types of energy as that found in electrical discharges. Over the millenia before life appeared, it seems that lightning could serve as the intermediary between simple molecules in the atmosphere and the production of nucleotides necessary for the synthesis of DNA and RNA. Thus, another problem solved, essential nucleotides must have been present on the surface of Earth in the days before the appearance of the first cells.

PROTEINS WOULD BE ESSENTIAL

While DNA provided stability for self replication, that would not be sufficient for the development of life, for that, proteins would be necessary. Proteins that could function as chemical agents, enzymes, to provide energy and assist in completing chemical reactions and assist in the synthesis of polymers of DNA and RNA. Proteins consist of long chains of amino acids bonded one to the other with a special "peptide" bond, so another problem needed a solution. Amino acids were needed to connect with the information contained in the nucleotide sequences in DNA. Did Earth, in its early days, have amino acids? The elegant work of Stanley Miller and Harold Urey has given definite information on how it may have been possible. They passed an electrical discharge through a gaseous mixture of methane, carbon dioxide, ammonia, hydrogen, and water, and found in the condensate several amino acids, acids that are found in the metabolic pathways of all living cells, and compounds that contained molecular groups that are known to be active in living cells. Under the influence of lightning bolts, amino acids were undoubtedly present on the surface of Earth not long after its formative days.

Over many millenia, lightning must have played a major role in the formation of deoxyribonucleotides, ribonucleotides, and amino acids. As simple organic compounds formed through the action of lightning bolts, they would undoubtedly accumulate on the surface of Earth and in pools of water, and by the continued action of lightning on accumulated compounds produce more complex molecules. There were no bacteria and less oxygen in the early atmosphere at the time of first DNA synthesis, so it would be very reasonable to assume that these early organic compounds could accumulate, concentrate and become more complex over the millennia before the appearance of the first living self propagating cell came into existence. In addition we must consider that lightning served as an intermediary between water, and rocks and soils of different kinds and the atmospheric gases that were providing carbon and nitrogen and possibly sulfur. The minerals and atoms in the rocks, soils, and water could serve as catalysts for bonding compounds into more complex and energetic forms with an accumulation over the surface after millions of years of interaction. In addition we must consider the lower levels of oxygen in the atmosphere until the first photosynthetic cells originated. Low levels of oxygen in the atmosphere could mean that an ozone layer was not present in the atmosphere high above Earth, so energetic ultraviolet rays and possibly low energy X-rays, could shower the surface and provide energy for the activation of atoms in molecules. Activated atoms could bond with other molecules to produce more complex compounds, or compounds with high energy, such as the phosphorylation of nucleotides to form nucleotide triphosphates, the high energy form of the nucleotides and the form that could store and release energy needed to drive synthetic processes. Nucleotide triphosphates would be the solution to another problem that faced life in its developmental stages. The triphosphates are also known to be a source of energy that exists in all cells living at the present time, and a source of energy that is used to bond one nucleotide to the next.

COMPONENTS NEEDED FOR PROTEIN SYNTHESIS

Amino acids were needed for the synthesis of proteins, but how did amino acids link together to form long polymers of amino acids that we know as proteins. For this I return to knowledge of the system that exists in all cells that live today. The synthesis of proteins is translated from DNA through an intermediary known as "messenger RNA". The nucleotides in a polymer of RNA match their complements in DNA, adenine in DNA transcribes to uracil in RNA, thymine in DNA to adenine in RNA, guanine in DNA to cytosine in RNA, and cytosine in DNA to guanine in RNA. The "messenger" binds to another component that contains two large molecules of RNA and a surrounding coat of protein, components known as ribosomes. The messenger moves through the ribosome and as it moves the code of every three nucleotides along the length of the messenger is translated to amino acids and one amino acid is bonded to another through a linkage known as a peptide bond. However, this is not the whole story, before the amino acids can bond to one another as the messenger RNA travels through the ribosome, each amino acid bonds to a small polymer of RNA called transfer RNA. Transfer RNA contains a sequence of three nucleotides that correspond to their complementary sequence in the messenger. The sequence of three recognizes its complement on the messenger, hydrogen bonds specifically to the sequence on the messenger, and transfers its amino acid to form a peptide bond with the previous amino acid, thus translating information from DNA to a developing protein with messenger RNA as an intermediary. The transfer and bonding of one amino acid to another while bound to transfer RNA and messenger RNA requires energy from a nucleotide triphosphate. On this basis, protein synthesis would require the presence of high energy nucleotides in the early environment of earth. These are the basics of protein synthesis as we know them today. However, this system specifies the presence of proteins on ribosomes, but supposedly, complex proteins have not been synthesized at this point in the development of life. One, two, or three amino acids may have been joined through the action of lightning and ultraviolet rays but nothing related to the triplet codes in large molecules DNA or RNA.

THE FIRST DNA POLYMER

This raises the question, could protein synthesis take place in the absence of ribosomes as we know them? I picture a hotter Earth on which deoxyribonucleotides, ribonucleotides, and amino acids have become concentrated over several thousand millenia. As these life sustaining molecules condensed out of the atmosphere they also removed carbon dioxide, methane and other carbon containing molecules from the atmosphere. Reduction of these "hot house gases" from the atmosphere permitted some cooling of the surface of the Earth and the retention of large puddles of water. Nucleotides and amino acids accumulated in the puddles and phosphates and sulfur were provided by rocks and soil. The action of ultraviolet rays and lightning could have activated phosphate molecules and bonded them to the sugars in the nucleotides and bonded one sugar to another to link one nucleotide to the next and over the mellenia produce a polymer of DNA. The ribose nucleotides were undoubtedly competing with deoxyribose nucleotides as the hereditary unit, but the unerring hydrogen bonding between adenine and thymine, and cytosine and guanine proved to be more stable and provided the stability that permitted one nucleotide to form a phosphate linkage to another nucleotide and eventually a large double stranded DNA polymer.

SYNTHESIS OF DNA AND "MESSENGER" RNA

This doesn't tell us how to proceed from DNA to a protein in the absence of ribosomes. Here I invoke environmental factors. With condensation of small carbon containing molecules from the atmosphere, the earth cooled to permit standing puddles of fresh water. It cooled to the point of being cold at night and hot during the day. Picture a big puddle of water containing concentrated deoxyribonucleotides, ribonucleotides, amino acids, and small and large polymers of double stranded DNA in a cool puddle. We know that double stranded DNA will separate into two polymers when heated to its melting point. Heating above this point will retain the two strands as single polymers, but cooling below this point will permit the two polymers to bond together to reform double stranded DNA. With this in mind, the puddle would heat up during the day and yield complements of single stranded DNA, and cool at night to reform double stranded DNA. During the hot phase, nucleotides, both phosphorylated deoxyribo- nucleotides and ribonucleotides, could hydrogen bond to their complements on the single stranded DNA. This would hold individual nucleotides in close proximity to one another, and through the action of lightning and ultraviolet rays activate the phosphates and sugars to form sugar-phosphate bonds between neighboring nucleotides, thus, forming polymers that would be complementary to the original single stranded DNA molecule. If this bonding was between ribonucleotides, the result would be an RNA polymer with nucleotides sequenced complementary to those of DNA. This would be equivalent to a molecule of "messenger RNA" that could be used for translation into a protein. If the bonding was between deoxyribo-nucleotides, the result would be another strand of DNA that would be complementary to the original, or a transcription of the original that could remain bonded to the original to form a double strand of DNA. Thus, the solution to two more problems, the replication of DNA and the synthesis of RNA from a template of DNA to form "messenger RNA" without the aid of polymerase enzymes.

THE IMPORTANCE OF CYCLIC TEMPERATURE

A cycle of temperature change would be important for hydrogen bonding between the nucleotides and their complements on the strand of DNA. If the temperature were too hot, it would prevent hydrogen bonding altogether, and if it remained cold, double stranded DNA would remain double stranded and not available for replication or for the synthesis of messenger RNA. With a cycle of temperature fluctuation, temperatures ideal for hydrogen bonding deoxyribonucleotides to single stranded DNA and ribonucleotides to single stranded DNA would be met twice a day. With different ideal bonding temperatures deoxyribo nucleotides could hydrogen bond to DNA at one time during the hot cold cycle and ribonucleotides could bond at another time. Both DNA and RNA could be synthesized from the same DNA template but at different times in the cycle.

FROM MESSENGER TO PROTEIN WITHOUT RIBOSOMES

Now that we have "messenger RNA" from a DNA template, how do we get from the messenger to a protein? First we need the small molecular forms of RNA, transfer RNA, that bonds to amino acids and has the triplet nucleotide sequence that will recognize its complementary triplet sequence in the messenger RNA. We know that all RNA is derived from a DNA template, so we need at least twenty small polymers of DNA that will transcribe into small polymers of RNA, and twist and turn and hydrogen bond within its own structure. Small polymers of RNA were no doubt abundant in the days when small polymers of DNA were abundant. Some of these small polymers might be capable of bonding to an amino acid with the aid of ultraviolet light and/or lightning. They would eventually contain a single stranded loop of RNA that would have a sequence of three nucleotide bases that would be complementary to three nucleotide bases in the "messenger RNA" molecule, and could hydrogen bond to those three bases. In the absence of ribosomes, messenger RNA would be floating around in water containing a concentration of amino acids bonded to transfer RNA, and the other ingredients needed for the development of life. At random, transfer RNA with bonded amino acid would hydrogen bond to its complement on the messenger, and another transfer RNA would hydrogen bond to the messenger, soon transfer RNA would hold adjacent amino acids in close proximity, ultra violet light, lightning, and perhaps one of the high energy ribonucleotide triphosphates would provide the energy to activate the amine group on one amino acid and the carboxyl group on the other amino acid to form a peptide bond that constitutes the linkage of one amino acid to the next in a protein. Energy from the same sources would simultaneously break the bond between transfer RNA and the amino acid. The chemistry of this scheme would require a two step process with at least two transfer RNAs that have an amino acid attached. First, one transfer RNA would hydrogen bond to the messenger, and a second transfer RNA would hydrogen bond to the messenger immediately adjacent to the first. Then the peptide bond would form and simultaneously break the bond between the first transfer RNA and its amino acid, in turn this would alter the configuration of the first transfer RNA and break the hydrogen bonding between the transfer RNA and the messenger and release the first transfer RNA from the messenger. This would make it possible for the next transfer RNA to hydrogen bond with the next triplet code on the messenger RNA, and add the next amino acid in the sequence. Without the aid of ribosomes and enzymes the synthesis would no doubt be slow but over the millenia it must have been possible.

THE FIRST PROTEIN: DNA POLYMERASE?

The first proteins to be synthesized would probably not be functional, but if the first protein to be functional was a DNA polymerase, the enzyme that links one deoxyribonucleotide to another, that one enzyme could replicate the DNA from which it was derived and increase the probability that more DNA polymerase molecules would be synthesized. There would be an explosion of enzymatically enhanced self-replicating DNA which could also replicate other DNA molecules. The number of DNA molecules would increase dramatically, this in turn would increase the probability that other functionally active nucleotide sequences would be introduced. The sequences that could serve as the templates for the synthesis of at least twenty transfer RNAs could easily be present in the billions of smaller DNA molecules that would be present in puddles spread over the surface of the earth.

THE ENHANCEMENT OF RNA AND PROTEIN SYNTHESIS

DNA molecules that could serve as the templates for at least twenty different transfer RNAs should be present in the primordial puddle otherwise synthesis of complete proteins would not be possible. The presence of another protein, RNA polymerase, the enzyme that polymerizes ribonucleotide sequences from a DNA template, would greatly enhance the transcription of RNA from DNA. Transfer RNAs and messenger type RNAs would undoubtedly be present among the billions of transcribed DNA molecules. One of the messengers at some time must have the sequence of nucleotides that would contain the code for the protein, RNA polymerase. The presence of this enzyme would enhance the synthesis of transfer RNAs and messenger RNAs from a DNA template, and continue to enhance the pathway that would lead to the enzymatic synthesis of proteins. What more is required? DNA molecules that code for the translation of the enzymes that attach amino acids to transfer RNAs, and enzymes that aid in the formation of peptide bonds after amino acid bonded transfer RNAs have hydrogen bonded to their proper code on the messenger RNA. The presence of all of these components in the primordial puddle could readily lead to the enzymatic synthesis of proteins that could aid in the synthesis of DNA, RNA, and more proteins that would all be relatively stable in an environment free of any type of organism.

THE SYNTHESIS OF MEMBRANE CONSTITUENTS

This primary protein synthetic mechanism would at first aid in the self-replication of DNA, but over the millennia the DNA molecules would be altered by the action of cosmic rays, X-rays, ultraviolet light and natural radioactivity that would alter the sequence of nucleotide bases in DNA. By chance some altered sequences would have to give rise to enzymes that would be involved with the synthesis of fatty acids and lipids. No living organisms would be present to synthesize fatty acids and lipids, so a mechanism for the synthesis of these compounds would have to be present before

DNA, RNA, and protein synthetic systems could be incorporated into or surrounded by membranes. Fatty acids and lipids would have to be present because they are essential for the formation of membranes; membranes that surround cells, membranes that constitute mitochondria, and membranes that incorporate a photosynthetic system to utilize a natural source of energy, light from the sun.

THE IMPORTANCE OF RIBOSOMES

The planet Earth would now have solutions to problems involved with the development of self-replicating DNA, the transcription of RNAs from DNA templates, and the translation of nucleotide triplets in "messenger RNA" into proteins. An advancement would be the development of ribosomes and the association of "messenger RNA" with ribosomes and their greatly enhanced ability to translate nucleotide triplets in the messengers into proteins. I don't believe that the two large RNA molecules in ribosomes and their associated proteins were present before living cells came into existence. The presence of ribosomes would be another solution to a problem, very slow translation of "messenger RNA" into proteins, ribosomes and their associated enzymes would rapidly bind messengers and rapidly translate their triplet sequences into proteins. Ribosomes would be enzyme units specifically designed for translation of messenger RNA into protein. Ribosomes would require two very large molecules of DNA for transcription of two very large RNA molecules, and more very large DNA molecules, their "messenger RNA" counter parts for translation into large proteins and associated enzymes. These points make me think that ribosomes probably didn't develop until living cells came into existence.

THE FORMATION OF MICELLES

The purpose of life is to solve problems, so the next step would be the incorporation of primordial puddle contents, all DNAs, all RNAs, nucleotides, and amino acids, inside structures that resemble the plasma membranes of cells. The basic structure of plasma membranes consists of bipolar molecules, one end is hydrophobic and the other end is hydrophyllic. The hydrophobic end contains chains of carbon atoms that are attracted to one another and are known to contain lipids. The hydrophobic end repels water. The hydrophyllic end contains a carbon based acid, a fatty acid, that is bonded to the hydrophobic chain of carbon, thus a bipolar molecule. In the presence of water the hydrophobic ends repel water and in so doing align themselves with one hydrophobe next to another and the hydrophyllic end aligns with other hydrophyllic ends. The surface tension created between the hydrophobic groups and the water bends these structures into tiny fluid filled spheres known as micelles with the hydrophobic end to the outside and hydrophyllic end to the inside. So, the formation of micelles in primordial puddles would incorporate DNA, RNA, nucleotides, and amino acids, all the contents of the puddles, inside the micelles, so the formation of micelles would be a very important step in the development of the first living organisms.

Micelles also solve another problem, the origin of a plasma membrane. The bipolar molecules lining the surface of a micelle resemble a basic plasma membrane of a cell and could help retain water within the micelle, and prevent the entrance of atoms and molecules that might be harmful. The micelle membrane would also help stabilize the water on the inside and should serve as a semi-permeable membrane to help prevent rapid changes in salt concentration in the water on the inside.

THE IMPORTANCE OF MICELLES

Up to the development of micelles, the chemistry for the development of life took place out in the open, in puddles, lakes, and oceans. The results of the chemistry were open to dilution, transport, and mixing with favorable and unfavorable conditions. We could call this era in the development of the chemistry of life Natures Test Tube Test For The Chemistry Of Life. Even after the formation of micelles, this same type of chemistry probably continued for a long long time, even in the micelles, until a mechanism for the equal distribution of DNA in budding micelles arose. This would signal a new era for molecular biology within the confines of cells, an era denoted by very rapid changes in the chemistry of life for laying the foundations for all the basic biochemical pathways found in life.

THE INITIATION OF CELL DIVISION

Now life needed to solve the problem of the equal distribution of DNA in a budding micelle. For this puddles rich in DNA, RNA, nucleotides, amino acids and a protein synthesizing mechanism, would be best. I say "puddles" because this would be where these materials could accumulate and concentrate through evaporation. The formation of micelles within these puddles would encapsulate a concentration of these important systems within a micelle. Incorporation into the confined space of a micelle would increase the probability that these systems could become synchronized to develop a mechanism for the equal distribution of DNA when one micelle budded into two. At first the micelles may have simply increased in size with the synthesis of DNA, RNA, and proteins. Upon reaching a certain volume one micelle simply broke into two with no regard to the distribution of DNA. With billions of micelles present in the waters of early Earth, one may have synthesized contractile proteins that would bond to one strand of a DNA molecule and another contractile protein that bonded to the other strand. Each of these proteins would have to bond to specific gel proteins located in opposite halves of a micelle. The contraction of these proteins would be synchronized with a band of contractile proteins that encircled the middle of the micelle. These proteins would be attached to a thin layer of gel proteins that go around the micell right under the bipolar membrane that forms the outer wall of the micelle. The completion of the synthesis of the second strand of DNA would trigger the contraction of all contractile proteins. The band of proteins around the middle of the micelle would contract to bring the outer walls to the center, thus dividing the micelle into two, while the proteins attached to the DNA would contract and pull one strand into one of the new micelles and the other strand into the other micelle. This would synchronize budding of the micelle into two, DNA synthesis, and the equal distribution of DNA to both buds. In the words of modern biology, cell division would be initiated for the first time. It would only have to happen in one micelle out of billions and billions over millions of years and the first self-replicating units would come into existence.

If one micelle did form a bud in synchrony with DNA synthesis then that would mean that the mechanism for one form of cell division had been established. For all practical purposes those micelles should be looked upon as bacteria, and they should continue to bud into a uniform population as long as the appropriate nutrients were available. The introduction of cell division would solve the problem of the perpetuation of cells over long periods of time, more or less forever, and establish the concept that all cells originate from previously existing cells.

CHANGES IN DNA BRING ADVANTAGEOUS DEVELOPMENTS

Now changes in DNA could take place in the confined space of "bacteria". Advantageous changes would not be dispersed into the general DNA population of a primordial puddle, a lake, or an ocean but retained within the bacteria and passed on to the budding siblings. There would undoubtedly be many deleterious changes but those would not survive and would be eliminated from the population. With a thin atmosphere, very little oxygen and no ozone layer, radiation from the sun, cosmic rays from outer space, and radioactive minerals on Earth would readily supply an intense level of radiation. Then, with the growth of billions of bacteria, and their dispersal to distant places, changes with a selective advantage could take place fairly rapidly. Development of a protective coat of materials outside the bipolar membrane of these early bacteria, and the development of a more sophisticated plasma membrane would be advantageous. The development of a more efficient mechanism for translation of "messenger RNAs" into proteins would enhance the ability to adapt quickly to changes that took place in DNA. The solution to rapid translation of RNAs came with the development of ribosomes, they very efficiently translate "messenger RNAs" into proteins but require amino acids bonded to transfer RNAs, so it would be advantageous to develop enzymes that would enhance the bonding of amino acids to transfer RNAs. I don't think that we will ever know if ribosomes came into existence all at once or if they developed in small increments over a long period of time. We do know that bacteria of the present day have ribosomes, so they must have developed at a very early stage in the history of life. Not knowing their exact origin should not distract from their importance to life. Their development would solve a big problem in the synthesis of proteins and further show that the purpose of life is to solve problems.

To think, the DNA in these first bacteria would ultimately give rise to all the plants and animals that have ever inhabited the Earth.

DEVELOPMENT OF A PHOTOSYNTHETIC SYSTEM

The most advantageous system that could arise at this time would be the inauguration of a system that would utilize the sun as a source of energy. The fossil record shows that the first bacteria appeared on Earth some 3.8 billion years ago, that was only 700 million years after the formation of the Earth. The microfossil record also shows that the cyanobacteria made their appearance on earth 3.7 billion years ago, so it only took 100 million years for the development of a system that could absorb photons from the sun and convert that energy into the synthesis of a sugar that could be used as a source of energy. The original bacteria must have developed a system that could absorb photons and convert that energy to a form that could be used in a biological system and those bacteria must have developed into the cyanobacteria.

The photosynthetic bacteria or the blue-green algae, the cyanobacteria, should have considerable advantage over bacteria that were dependent on metabolizable chemicals. Bacteria that were reliant on sulfur as a source of energy would be limited to places at which sulfur was present in the appropriate form and concentration. The early bacteria that were dependent on organic chemicals would be dependent on the source and location of those chemicals. This would have to be other bacteria that had died and released their molecules into the environment, no other forms of life would have been present, or organic molecules that would originate when lightening struck in an atmosphere with a high carbon content. The organisms with photosynthetic capability could disperse to every niche that had light from the sun, sufficient water, and a source of nitrogen, phosphorous, and sulfur. That would include the first few feet of the ocean surface and that surface covered the vast majority of the Earth, so the cyanobacteria could disperse over most of the surface of the Earth and onto moisture laden places on the land.

The cyanobacteria would have very little competition from other organisms and would undoubtedly proliferate rapidly. They might even use up the nutrients that had accumulated from lightning strikes over the past thousands of millenia. This great development of photo-synthesizing cyanobacteria could rapidly change Earth's atmosphere. When photosynthetic organisms metabolize the sugar that was made during photosynthesis, they give off a molecule of oxygen, so ocean and land covered with cyanobacteria could produce many molecules of oxygen and rather rapidly change the atmosphere to one containing enough oxygen to support air breathing animals.

DNA: THE ULTIMATE SOLUTION TO LIFE'S PROBLEMS

Two more problems solved, how to utilize a constant free source of energy through photosynthesis and the dispersal of a changeable retainable form of DNA over the entire surface of the Earth. This would permit cells to colonize every permissible niche of sea and land. Now it was a matter of waiting for changes in DNA that would not be lethal, the changes would have to promote adaptations to new environments and continued advances and refinements in biochemistry. This would lead to the great diversity of plant and animal life that has come into existence on Earth over a span of at least 3.8 billion years.

Ultimately, changes in DNA that permitted adaptations to varied environments would lead to the solutions of problems that would permit the development of very diverse plant and animal populations that could inhabit every habitat on Earth, and this all originated with the solution to the first problem, the development of a large organic molecule that could be precisely replicated, that could contain information that could be stored through many replications, that could be altered ever so slightly thus permitting the production of new proteins that could be duplicated if they proved to be advantageous, or eliminated if they did not contribute to survival. These are all properties of DNA, the solution to the basic problem facing the development and perpetuation of all life, and the solution to the problems of life after the dispersal of DNA in organisms that could be considered living.

LIFE IN COMPLEX SOCIETIES

Thus far, concern has been with developments in the chemistry of life and how developments in chemistry solved problems that eventually led to organisms that could be considered bacteria, and in turn the DNA in these first living organisms was modified to give rise to all the plants and animals on planet Earth. This also showed that developments in the chemistry of life answered the question: "what is the purpose of life?", by solving problems that led to the first living forms that could be sustained. For life and its development, solutions to these problems would be the most important, but would the question, "what is the purpose of life", and the answer, "to solve problems", apply to life that has developed complex societies?

Modern humans have developed the most complex societies, so a list of some of the problems that humans have solved would be in order. The list is actually endless because humans continue to answer the question about the purpose of life and continue to solve problems as they advance through life, their ability to solve problems is their great achievement. I shall include a few problems that have been solved by the great apes and early hominids to show that this trait undoubtedly began before modern humans entered the scene.

Let us take a brief look at chimpanzees, as non-human primates they have solved a few interesting problems. They use sticks as weapons to ward off predators and to hit one another in fights and they throw stones. Using sticks and stones solves the problem of hurting their hands by hitting and avoiding close contact with an enemy that might bite. They solved the problem of avoiding raindrops by turning large leaved vegetation into umbrellas. They use tools to process food. They have solved the problem of procuring termites by using grass straws and they use stones to break open nuts. Except for the use of straws and large leaves, chimps problems involved pain and the solutions that they worked out involved the use of tools that would let them avoid pain.

If chimpanzees learned to solve a few of their problems, there is no reason to believe that human's most distant ancestor, <u>Orrorin tugenensis</u>, a hominid who lived six million years ago, didn't solve some of its problems by developing more sophisticated techniques than those used by chimpanzees. Orrorin is only known through fossils and didn't leave any tools so it is difficult to say that they lived a more complex life than Chimps. The same would have to be said of the next group of hominids, the Auatralopithicenes who are known to have lived from 4.4 million years ago to 2 million years ago. *Homo habilis* is believed to have arisen from the Australopithicenes and lived from 2 million years ago to 1.5 million years ago. *Homo habilis* was the first hominid to leave stone tools at the sites where their fossil bones have been found, so Habilis must have solved some of its problems by making stone tools.

HOUSING

First a look at chimps and gorillas, they don't make their own houses but they do make beds. Before it gets dark they pull vegetation together to make beds that they will use for sleep. This might be considered the first house, they made it purposely, probably gives some protection, and it will house them during sleep at night. The early hominids probably made similar beds but there is no indication that later hominids added to their own protection until neanderthals and modern humans started using caves for houses. After that humans started making their own shelters and huts, and these grew into villages with houses. Through the ages, humans continued to solve their housing problems to include the development of giant sky-scrapers found in the complexities of large cities. Of course it took the development of engineering and engineers, and the invention of many gadgets to accomplish this but humans have solved all the problems that came along and today we see the results in skyscrapers over a thousand feet tall.

TRANSPORTATION

Transportation has gone from walking and running with two legs, to riding horses and horse drawn carts, to the development of trains, automobiles, buses, trucks, and airplanes. Think of all the problems that had to be solved in the development of these items. As a corollary to transportation, paths and walkways had to be cleared for walking and running, stables and feed had to be maintained for horses, roads had to be built and train tracks had to be laid, a system of highways and interchanges had to be built and fuel stations supplied for automobiles, buses, and trucks; airplanes required airports, fuel, and unerring communication networks. All had problems that living humans solved.

COMMUNICATION

Communication started with body language, grunts, groans, and roars before the development of language, but after language developed humans in close contact talked, shouted at a distance and yelled over longer distances. Then humans developed techniques of tapping on wood and drums to solve the problem of communication at distances beyond sight. Then a human discovered that a static electrical signal could be sent over copper wires and a message could be sent with long and short static pulses standing for letters of the alphabet and the telegraph came into existence. This made long distance communication possible and the railroads put it to immediate use. Soon after the telegraph, Alexander Graham Bell found that vibrations of the human voice could be used to generate electrical impulses that could be transmitted through copper wires. The impulses could be sent long distances and used to vibrate a speaker that would make the same sounds as those that generated the impulses. People could talk to one another over telephones, and this solved many personal problems and business problems, but it also created another industry that needed solutions to many problems. With solutions to problems in electronics, telephones moved on to use electromagnetic waves and satellites to reconstruct the human voice, so wires were no longer needed, telephones became wireless and loaded with electronic media.

MEDIA

Media in both the new world and old started as carvings in stone, paintings on walls and in caves, designs on clay pots, and marks on clay tablets. Humans had to solve the problem of how to carve stone, what could be used as paint, how it could be applied, and what would make fast distinct marks in clay. Stone, walls, pots, and tablets were all very good sites for the first media because they would last a long time but they were very bulky and not useful for every day communication. Humans solved the bulk problem with the invention of paper and that required solutions to even more problems. A solution to the rapid manufacture of paper had to be found to keep up with demand, and printing presses had to be invented to keep up with the demand for written and pictorial material. Film for an optical system, the camera, was developed and this brought cheap almost instant pictures to newspapers, magazines, and families. People wanted to make their own pictures so quantities of cameras and film had to be manufactured. Motion pictures came into existence not long after the development of film. This brought cameramen, actors and actresses, directors, and writers to the scene, and eventually the development of elaborate movie studios that employed thousands of people. Then came radios with waves transmitted through the sky and picked up by a receiver and amplified so that humans could hear the sounds coming from a box. This presented a whole new set of problems that needed human solutions. Radios had to be manufactured, radio advertising came into existence, radio programs needed voices and stars, writers were needed, music was played and musicians, conductors, and song writers were needed; and stations needed operators and announcers. Television came along with a set of problems similar to those of motion pictures and radio, and solutions to those problems were found. The digital processing of information by computers was never related to developments in television but rather to business and the military. The population of the world was climbing steadily, paper work was becoming a burden and falling behind the task of keeping up-to-date records, military records, equipment, and strategy were moving at a pace that required more than paper, all major problems that needed solutions. The first digital computer came along and it didn't do very much, the second appeared and it didn't do very much either, but the third came with storage, a word processor and a printer. The solution to three problems in one little box. It was goodbye to typewriters, digital computers were needed by business and education in particular and they sold in record numbers for the next ten years. Solutions to all types of problems were being solved with new hardware and software. Totally unforeseen solutions to problems were being handled by computers and everyone had to have at least one. Computer based applications came into existence, software engineers were writing programs to solve all types of problems so sales of applications along with computers advanced for another ten years. During this same time computer games were under development and machines based on computer hardware were being devoted to action games, and here, graphic designers were needed to develop figures and background, for reality kinesiologists studied human motion, and software engineers put it together for those seeking action packed games. In the meantime, the military was solving their communication problems by developing a network of cables that connected all military bases and command operations, and then brought in connections to universities, they called it the "internet". This solved the military problem and gave them direct connections to advanced knowledge at universities, but a few years later they released the "internet" to the public. Corporations immediately adapted the system to telephone lines that were already in place so the "internet" was open to world wide communication for the cost of a local telephone call. An immediate solution to cheap world wide communication. Modems connected computers to the internet and they sold briskly for a time. Hundreds of thousands of people thought that they were going to get rich by selling things on the internet. They set themselves up with high capacity digital storage space to handle the sales, money transactions, advertising, and shipping, and paid their employees with stock options. Things really boomed for the digital industry for a couple of years while everyone was getting things set up, but it came time for sales and very few people went to the internet to buy the items that they needed. The so called dot coms (.com) didn't last long, they all failed, the stock with which they paid employees was worthless. Even well established retail stores tried it on a minor level and it didn't work for them either. I predicted to myself that people would not buy the things that they needed over the internet and they didn't. The human factor was totally overlooked, humans like to look, touch, feel, inspect, try on and try out the things that they need, want, buy. I wouldn't think of buying a big red raw steak unless I took a good long look at it, or a new jacket, or a new pair of shoes. If I choose it, it becomes personal. If a store clerk chooses it, it gains no personal meaning. The "dot com bust", as it is called, is an illustration of a choice that did not match the purpose of life, so did not solve a human problem, but created many hardships for the people working the dot coms, for shippers, and for the suppliers of the electronic equipment.

EDUCATION

Education is another area that began before hominids entered the picture of life on Earth. We know that a troop of rhesus monkeys living near the seashore in Japan were given sweet potatoes placed on a sandy beach. The monkeys liked the sweet potatoes but not the sand. One day a female with a baby took a potato out to the water and washed it in the water before biting into it, no more sand. She relayed the technique to her baby and to other members of the troop, soon the entire troop was washing their potatoes, and have passed the information to succeeding generations. Another problem solved through experimentation and education. I mentioned another instance of learning in rhesus monkeys living on an island off the coast of Puerto Rico. These troops treat the scale insects that live on the rocks in a tidal lagoon as a delicacy. They patiently pick these tiny specks off the rocks one at a time and transfer them to their lips. These rhesus were not native to the island but placed there by humans for study, so they had to learn to eat the scale insects on their own. With the great apes, older chimpanzees teach the younger chimps to probe for termites with grass straws, to throw rocks, and to make umbrellas and beds. Gorillas and chimps learn a sign language, and orangutans teach their young to mimic, to climb, and which vegetation to eat. From the monkeys and apes we have to surmise that the very early hominids, Orrorin and the australopithicenes, had the abilities of the monkeys and great apes and perhaps more, so they must have taught their offspring things that would have survival value or we wouldn't be here today. The first hominids known to manufacture stone tools in abundance, *Homo habilis*, must have passed their techniques to friends and relatives because the same types of tools have been found wherever Habilis has been found. Furthermore, the manufacture of stone tools by each successive hominid, like *Homo erectus*, *Homo ergastor*, *Homo antecessor*, *Homo heidelbergensis*, *Homo neanderthalensis*, and *Homo sapiens*; became more sophisticated, more fine tuned, and expanded in type. From the fossil records of the tools, it doesn't appear that each new group went back to the primary tools of Habilis, and started over again from there and worked their way into new more sophisticated designs. It looks as if each group started with more detailed designs and maintained those designs with modifications. To arrive at a new design without a trace of a previous design had to involve someone who knew what stones to choose and how to achieve the goal of stone tools that represented a group of hominids. This means that someone had technical information that was passed from one individual to another over time and through generations of time. Also, additions to that information had to be passed to succeeding generations, or they may have had to start all over again. This was a working educational system that lasted for eons and carried right on through to modern *Homo sapiens*, who developed ever more sophisticated tools. It solved the continued production of highly needed tools over long periods of time and lasted right through the development of civilizations. As a side note, *Homo erectus* seems to be the first to use fire, so information on control and how to start a fire and keep it burning must have been passed through generations. Information on paints, painting, and lighting the walls of the caves in France and Spain was worked out and must have been taught to generations of people because that activity continued for over ten thousand years. After the invention of written languages in Mesopotamia and Egypt, scribes had to learn how to write the language, do math, and teach others, so a more formal form of education came into existence. Through the dark ages and into the renaissance educational problems were solved by the clergy, with apprenticeships in specialized "guilds", or the hiring of private tutors by the elite. Most of the renaissance painters and sculptors learned through apprenticeships and by living in the palaces of very prominent families. Universities, mostly involved with religions, appeared in the twelve hundreds, but didn't solve very many secular problems. It wouldn't be until the fifteen hundreds and after the invention of the printing press that universities would begin involvement with secular problems. Here the discoveries of Isaac Newton and Galileo stand out as prominent figures in educational inquiry. Newton solved problems in math and explained the occurrence of physical phenomena on Earth and in the universe. Galileo's discoveries brought the wrath of religious thinkers, but solved a big problem that brought revolutionary thoughts; the Earth was not the center of the solar system (universe) but a mere planet in orbit around the Sun like other planets. After this universities became features of most countries, even the United States had its first university in the North with the establishment of Harvard in 1636, and its second, almost sixty years later, the College of William and Mary in Virginia in 1693. The establishment of universities in most countries involved governments that saw the need to extend education to their constituents and solved the problem of educating teachers who in turn would go out over the countryside, establish schools and bring education and knowledge to the people so that they would be prepared to fulfill their purpose in life, to solve problems.

INSTRUMENTS OF WAR

Instruments of war were always big items that required solutions. Chimpanzees and no doubt the early hominids solved the problem of weapons by using what was at hand, sticks and stones. *Homo habilis*, another early hominid, made stone axes and mallets that may have been hafted to wood handles, and undoubtedly used these instruments to fight predators. After *Homo habilis*, each successive group of hominids made more sophisticated stone weapons which became even more lethal with the invention of atlases, spears, bows, and arrows. Lethal instruments made of stone lasted for almost two million years but the next advance didn't come from stone but with solutions to the problems of how to work metals. Copper appears to have been the first that was shaped into a weapon but it was too soft to serve as an instrument of war. However, this problem was solved when other metals such as tin and nickel were added to molten copper to make bronze. It was hard and could be shaped and cast to make knives and daggers, and the sharp tips of arrows and spears. With experience at making bronze, smelting and working iron would be possible. Now whole armies could be supplied with swords, body armor, and lance and arrow tips made from iron. Powered by the discovery of explosives and dynamite, the development of steel brought better guns, rifles, cannons, bombs, armored tanks, and battle ships to the list of war instruments that would supposedly solve the problems of nations. The next war sought to solve problems with the development of radar, sonar, jet planes, subsonic and supersonic rockets, and atomic bombs that really did solve the problem of bringing World War II to an end. After this war, nations sought to solve international problems with the development of hydrogen bombs, inter-continental ballistic missiles, spy planes and orbiting satellites with ultra-super photography, supercomputers that could handle information on incoming and outgoing ballistic missiles, trips of man into orbit around Earth and to the Moon, the development of space shuttles that orbit the Earth, orbiting habitable space platforms, an orbiting space telescope, orbiting space probes that collect information on the origin of infrared light, x-Rays, and gamma rays; space probes sent to the planets and beyond, and the landing of robot machines on the surface of Mars to explore for water and more. All of the items after World War II would address the purpose of life by solving fairly specific problems of a military or a scientific nature, but their real significance abounds in the fact that numerous small problems had to be solved to bring these items to fruition, and it is the solutions to the smaller problems that brings new information, new ways of doing things, better approaches, and new ideas, and new machinery to humanity.

CONCLUSION

A look at a few more lists that could have been included, agriculture, chemistry, physics, and medicine. Think of the advances that have taken place in these fields over the years, and the problems that arose and had to be solved in a few more areas of human endeavor. With these partial lists of solutions that humans have brought to themselves over many millions of years, the evidence becomes overwhelming and serves as definitive proof that THE PURPOSE OF LIFE is now and always has been, TO SOLVE PROBLEMS, ever since the very first molecules of DNA became the foundation of life. Humans are happiest when they are finding solutions to problems.

Chapter 2

THE GODS OF HUMANS ARE HUMANS

YOUTHFUL PICTURES OF GOD

During my early childhood I wondered, who is this character called god? People whom I knew seemed to indicate that he was male, they always referred to god as he or him, said that he was a spirit or like a ghost, and indicated that he lived in the sky in a place called Heaven. My parents, friends and relatives had pictures of god and these made him appear as a strong old man with white hair and a white beard with a solid look of force in his face and great strength in a body that was definitely like that of the people I knew. He was dressed in white flowing robes or cloths that blended with white clouds and a blue sky. So, when I heard or saw a reference to god, this was the picture that came into my mind during childhood, a picture that was drawn from pictures that I had seen. As time passed into my teenage years, I learned a few more myths about god. I was told that god was a very powerful figure who created the earth, the sky, the moon, the universe, and all the people who lived on the Earth in the present and in the past, and those who would live on Earth in the future. I was told that god had the powerful ability to keep track of all the living people and the spirits of all the dead people who had passed his judgment and were permitted to enter his heaven, or were sent into the depths of the earth to a place called Hell, if they didn't pass his judgment as to whether they lived a good life or a life that didn't live up to his standards. I was told that god knew everything and controlled everything, he made the clouds, the rain, all the crops, the animals, the fish, and streams, even the birth and death of every person. These items were added to my picture of god when he appeared in my mind through my early teenage years.

It was also during my early teens that I came to understand the relation between god and Jesus and their relation to the old and new testaments. The old testaments were about god and his times and the new testaments were about Jesus and his times. I understood that Jesus was the son of god through his mother, the Virgin Mary. God fertilized Mary and she gave birth to Jesus while she was a virgin. I came to understand the stories of Christmas time, of Joseph and Mary traveling to Bethlehem, not finding a place to stay they took residence in a manger where Mary gave birth to Jesus, and three wise men from the East brought gifts for baby Jesus.

Now I developed a minds eye picture of Jesus that stemmed from a picture that my grandmother had hanging on the wall of the ranch in Atascadero. I wouldn't learn until much later that a real picture of Jesus did not exit, all pictures of Jesus were made in the minds of artists or in the minds of the people who commissioned the artists. My picture of Jesus was a man with a very kind but suffering look on his face, a man with a beard and a full head of brown hair, a man who existed only from the shoulders to the top of his head as in the picture on my grandmother's wall. I also had another picture of Jesus from pictures that I saw at the church that I frequented. This was a picture of Jesus nailed to a cross with blood dripping from his hands and feet, from a wound in his chest, and from the wounds caused by a halo of thorns pressed around his head. I also developed a moving three dimensional picture of Jesus from some of the great movies that involved his life. So, the picture of Jesus that I held in my mind was derived from pictures that I viewed and from stories that I learned, not from first hand knowledge.

WHERE IS HEAVEN AND WHO IS GOD?

During my early teenage years I frequented a Presbyterian Church in Atascadero, California. While at church I befriended the son of a deacon of the church, I believe that his name may have been Willard. One day I found myself isolated in one of the church school classrooms with Willard. He became very serious and started telling me about Jesus and asked if I knew that god sent his son to redeem the sins of the people. As he continued preaching about Jesus for the next few minutes, I became very uncomfortable and when he asked me, "do you believe that Jesus is our savior", I got very nervous and quickly replied, "yes"? At this time I was asking myself, what is this guy up to? He came back with a more relaxed tone, "I'm so glad that you accept Jesus Christ as your personal savior. Now you will have everlasting life and will go to heaven. Now you can become a full fledged member of the church." I said "yes, I believe in John 3:16", and stood up. Willard stood up too and gave me a big hug and now gave the appearance of being very happy about saving another person from purgatory. My thoughts were going in another direction, does this character actually think that that is all it takes to be saved, from what? As a young teen I didn't think that I had committed any great big sins. What are these sins that I am supposed to be saved from? I was going to high school and doing a good job there, I got up in the morning to catch the bus to school and brought good feelings to the other students on the bus, I took on the responsibility of milking four cows in the morning before school and in the evening after school, I kept my grandmother supplied with dry oakwood pieces for her wood burning stove, and drove my mother into town whenever she wanted to go. I was being a good naturally responsible kid. I didn't see very many sins going on in my life. Besides, I had to question, where is this great big place called heaven? I look up and what do I see, blue sky and stars and a sun and a moon, and clouds and lightning now and then. Heaven and god and Jesus and my dead relatives and all of my dead acquaintances will end up there somewhere?

After my encounter with Willard, I avoided him whenever I went to church. As a matter of fact, I seriously doubt that I ever exchanged words with him again. I absolutely did not appreciate his approach to "saving my soul", and definitely began to wonder who god might be and where did he reside? I continued to go to that church every now and then all through my days in high school but slowly drifted away by attending only a few Sundays during my senior year in high school.

A GLIMPSE INTO THE WORLDS RELIGIONS

BUDDHISM

My mental picture of god and who he might be expanded when I went to U.C., Berkeley. During my studies at the university I found that there were gods other than the Christian god, Jesus, and Mary, the gods that I pictured in my mind. I found that there was a spiritual leader who went by the name of Buddha. He was depicted as male and became the spiritual leader of the people of China, Japan, and Southeast Asia. I learned that Buddha was born in India and lived about five hundred years before Christ. Unlike the christian god, Buddha was human with all the characteristics of a human. Buddha's interest was in the relief of suffering and poverty, so he invented The Four Noble Truths and The Eightfold Path, which if followed would lead to Nirvana where death, reincarnation, and suffering no longer existed. Buddhists believe in reincarnation and that made it possible to have more than one Buddha over many many years and made it possible to add to or change the teachings of Buddha.

In my view Buddha was the most human spiritual leader with the stature of a god, so my knowledge now included two gods but that didn't help my understanding of who god might be.

JUDAISM

I was somewhat familiar with Judaism from studies on the Old Testament of the Bible but I wanted to know more so I looked deeper into the religion by talking to the Jewish people that I knew very well. I found that Abraham was a key figure, he was a man who talked to god and made an agreement with god. The children of Abraham and all of their relatives would be the "chosen" people of god. This meant that the Jewish people were the "chosen" people but I never did get an understanding of what this meant other than "gods chosen people". What did it mean to this god? To me this sounded like a self-fulfilling prophecy by Abraham, he chose his descendants to be the chosen people. I went on to learn that Abraham agreed with god to have his descendant's agree to "abide by the laws of god" and god promised that Abraham's descendants would develop into a great nation. Abraham's descendants settled in a place called Canaan, until it came into a great drought, and Jacob, a grandson of Abraham, and his family went to Egypt and Jacob's sons established the twelve tribes of Israel and did very well in Egypt until a pharaoh wanted to limit their numbers. After this, the Exodus from Egypt occurs and god gives His laws, the Ten Commandments, to Moses. These talks didn't help my understanding of god. God suddenly appears in the mind of Abraham and this becomes god. God tells Abraham and his descendants what to write, but it tells me nothing about god himself, he suddenly appears, tells how it all came into being, makes agreements, gives commands, and writes laws through his "chosen" people. This makes me believe that this god exists only in the minds of the people who wrote the words of this god.

By this time I was beginning to wonder if any religion could tell me who god might be, so I looked deeper into the religions that I heard about and found that no religion had an explanation for god other than that he existed as a supernatural spirit, had features like those of humans, and came from somewhere up in the sky when answering the calls of humans or delivering words of wisdom.

ISLAM

I heard that the Islamic religion was somewhat like that of the Bible and found that the Islamic god, called Allah, sent all of the prophets of the Bible to Earth so that they could deliver the words of god to the people on Earth. Thus, Muslims have faith in all the prophets and take their word as the word of god, but they believe that these words were distorted over the many years of their existence. So, Muslims take the word of the most recent prophet, Muhammad, born in Mecca, as the true word of god. Muhammad often went to Mount Hira to meditate on the many gods that were present in that part of the country and wondered who the true god might be. During one of his journeys to Mount Hira, Muhammad received a revelation from god. The revelation was delivered by the angel Gabriel, and later all of Muhammad's revelations were placed into writing as the Qur'an, which the Muslims take as the direct word of god. The life stories and sayings of Muhammad have been studied and authenticated, and became the Hadith, or rules that Muslims try to live by. The Qur'an and Hadith form the laws of Islam. Once again this didn't clarify my understanding of who god might be, god suddenly appeared to Muhammad to present his revelations to his most recent prophet.

DHARMA

I continued to expand my quest on the nature of god and looked into the Hindu world. I found that the people of India do not refer to their religion as Hindu but as "dharma" which means "law" or "social duty". It is a very old religion and goes back to the time when the Aryans came into India. It is interwoven into life in India, has hundreds of gods that developed over the years, and no books of belief that everyone should follow, but it has one unifying principle, a universal spirit that pervades all living things, perhaps a human spirit, it is this spirit that makes reincarnation possible. People are born, live on Earth, die, and are reborn, but each time they are reborn they must advance in order to attain oneness with their god. To advance, you must lead a good life, study the dharma texts, and obey the god of your choice through prayer, then you might become one with god. No clues as to the nature of god, but many descriptions of hundreds of gods, all with various attributes that will lead people to Nirvana, a world with no more cycles of birth, death, and rebirth.

YOGA

My first two years in graduate school, I delved into Yoga and Transcendental Meditation and found that neither had a god. I knew immediately that these religious forms wouldn't help answer my question about god, but perhaps the god that I was attempting to find didn't exist. These philosophies might point in another direction and give a clue as to where I might look for answers. My studies on Yoga told me that I had to watch for Fakirs and distinguish them from true Yoga Masters. Fakirs performed monumental tricks of the body and mind and proclaimed that their feats were possible because of their devotion to Yoga and practice of Yoga meditation, but in reality they were notable tricks for personal gain. Yoga Masters could control most of their bodily functions through meditation but they never used this ability for personal gain. Orderly control of physiological functions was a step toward their ultimate goal, to attain complete control of the body and mind in order to transcend from the body into a world of timelessness. In this world they could travel over the world, collect information and advance their thinking, but had to seek another, more advanced, human body after a period of time. The knowledge that they gained in the timeless world was used in the real world to advance humankind after they returned to the real world in a new body. These people would eventually become the great thinkers, artists, writers, innovators, inventors, political leaders of the world. In the timeless world, Yogas traveled about and could see where advances were needed, not necessarily monumental advances but simple advances that could benefit humanity. After returning to a human body, a Yoga could put these advances into practice. These are very noble thoughts on how advances might be made and may foretell genetics and evolution as we know them today. In my searches through Yoga I never came across a timeline for time in the timeless world. Could it be as short as a few milliseconds? In which case it might be equivalent to insight or enlightenment, we work on a difficult problem without reaching a solution for some time, we turn away for a few brief seconds, suddenly we have the solution. Could this be after a brief excursion into the timeless world? Like the Hindus, Yogas believe in a form of reincarnation, but unlike the Hindus, gods are not involved, perhaps the timeless world could be considered a god.

TRANSCENDENTAL MEDITATION

My studies of Transcendental Meditation led me to find that it was similar to Yoga meditation but reincarnation was never involved. One learned to control bodily functions through meditation. Eventually, mental control would reach the point where you could leave the body and travel into space, but you would return to your own body for nourishment and replenishment. At first you could only make brief excursions into the transcendental world, but with each excursion you could remain in the transcendental state for longer periods of time. The ultimate goal was to achieve supreme control in the transcendental state and remain in a world of everlasting sunsets and total bliss with absolutely no need for life on the surface of the Earth. Supposedly, in the transcendental state you would be able to give help to humanity for life in a world of peace, tranquility, charm, and love.

Both Yoga and Transcendental Meditation didn't appear to involve gods, only humans with the ability to use meditation to control the mind and transport it into a world conceived by the mind itself. My studies of Yoga and Transcendental Meditation left me with abilities to control many of my bodily functions to the benefit of my personal health, but we control numerous bodily functions on a daily basis, defecation and urination as obvious examples. We don't defecate or urinate right at the time that the body tells us that it is time to eliminate waste products from our bodies. Most of the time we control these functions until we arrive at a time that is more suitable or convenient. Extend the ability to control these two bodily functions to the heart, blood vessels, and lungs, and you readily control the heart beat, blood pressure, and rate of breathing, or the amount of oxygen that enters your blood stream and is delivered to your tissues. Extend the ability to control these functions to other functions and you enter the world of Yoga Masters and the ultimate in Transcendental Meditation, here the invocation of a god other than yourself does not appear to be necessary. My grand conclusion for Yoga and Transcendental Meditation was that they are forms of self-hypnosis. Under self-hypnosis a person could direct their mind into a world that transcends the body and becomes a world of the mind, or a world under the control and direction of the mind. In that way, persons could believe that their minds could transcend their body into the timeless world established by thoughts from the brain.

A CHERISHED HUMAN CONCEPT

After my studies on Yoga and Transcendental Meditation, I thumbed through several encyclopedias on religion to look into the basic philosophy behind the worlds more obscure religions. Just as the major religions, I found that they too offered some form of life after death, this appears to be central to the philosophy of all religions. Furthermore, in my studies of these encyclopedias I looked for descriptions of gods, not descriptions of what they did or could do, or purpose, but descriptions of who they might be, where they resided, did they consist of something other than spirit, was there a description of what the spirit might be? Of course, it was rather futile to think that I might find clues to the answers to these questions. Most gods are assumed to be omnipotent and omnipresent, ready to answer at any moment with no physical identity. Accordingly, these studies did not reveal the nature of the world's gods, but they did reveal an ability that led to more questions. The ability was the almost universal ability of gods to create both spiritual and materialistic items. Where and how do gods get energy or power for their creations, and where do they get materials for their materialistic creations? What is the origin of their creative ideas? I would suggest that the ideas have human origin, the creations of the gods satisfy human needs. I use the plural because many different gods of humans have the ability to create the same earth, the same plants, the same animals, the same humans, provide similar laws, and similar tasks. Thus, the gods of humans give humans a place to live, provide plants and animals for food and amusement, provide order, and tasks that will challenge human brain power, and one more most important proviso, the gods of humans give humans a form of life after death. It seems that all of the gods who have existed in the history of humans appear to give humans something that is very basic to the health of the human spirit. The gods appeal to humans? Follow the path of the words that I give you and you shall have life after your death. A concept that is cherished by humans, a concept that makes death bearable and life possible, a human concept that is accepted and needed by practically all humans who have ever existed.

THE NATURE OF THE GODS OF HUMANS

It seems that humans invented gods who were shaped and molded by the minds of humans. Thus, humans invented gods that could not write because their gods were not physically endowed with hands and fingers, only spiritually endowed. Supposedly the hands and fingers of their gods were spirits that could not hold pens or pencils, if pens and pencils existed at the time humans invented their gods. Writing implements did not exist at the time most gods were invented so the gods of most humans were not endowed with the ability to write. Besides, we must take into consideration, very few humans could write at the time that they invented their gods. Humans did not give their gods the ability to write, but they gave their gods the ability to think and speak. This gave humans the ability to communicate with the gods that they invented. Thus, humans could claim that they were writing words on behalf of their gods, gods defined by the humans who were writing for the gods of humans. According to this reasoning, the gods of humans are humans themselves. Thus, all humans are gods and all of the gods of humans are humans, and this extends back to the time that a human first thought that a fellow human should be buried after death, for this was when humans began to think that a human life was more valuable than they witnessed during the life of the individual being buried. We must extend his life and think that this human will live on after his death in the land of a spirit, the land of a god, this brings comfort to our minds.

Humans have invented their gods in the image of humans so they have defined human characteristics. Humans have given their gods the ability to think, to reason, to express feeling, to give help, to give health, to bring harm, to bring death, to bring happiness and love; all everyday occurrences in the lives of humans. However, humans have not endowed their gods with physical attributes. Humans have not given their gods a physical brain with which to think, express, reason, and feel. To reiterate, humans have not given their gods the ability to write, if the gods of humans had the ability to write, wouldn't the gods write their own laws, commands, orders of life, directly, themselves, and command subservient humans to obey the writing? (Supernatural gods should have the ability to write otherwise the supernatural gods would not be able to instruct humans on how to write the many languages that they know. If humans did not have the ability to write, then they would not be able to write the words passed on to humans by their supernatural gods.) This would eliminate human's communication with human gods, and humans ability to write words of law and order and life as befit the human who was writing words of wisdom in the name of a god. Thus, a human who learned to write could assume the nature of god and say that human writing was the word of god when a supernatural god passed them on to me to write in his name, but in reality, they are the words of a human, my words. If the gods of humans were humans, and humans wrote the words of gods, then the words of humans would be the words of the gods of humans. In other words, humans would be writing the words of humans and the words of gods, all humans should consider themselves humans and gods, that would make the gods of humans, humans. That being the case, the words that I write are the words of a human god, the source of the words, human thought, therefore, the writing of a human.

DID A GOD CREATE THE UNIVERSE?

One of the most universal attributes of most of the gods of humans is the ability to create the universe. This creates the question, did a god create the universe or did humans create the gods who created the universe, or did the universe and solar system arise from purely physical phenomena? According to cosmological evidence, our universe was created some fourteen and a half billion years ago out of a spark known as the "big bang". That spark rapidly expanded and filled a vacuum with matter that would eventually coalesce into stars, galaxies, planets, moons, "dark matter", "dark energy", and much later supernovae that would supply the universe with the required heavier atomic elements. Where would a god enter the cosmological picture? Humans studying cosmology have physically explained the evolution of the cosmos without the interjection of a god or gods to explain the origin and fate of our universe. So far, the continued expansion of the universe has not been satisfactorily explained physically or mathematically, but the recent discovery of dark matter and dark energy could readily explain the continued expansion of the universe without the invocation of a god, the god that oversees the expansion of the universe. The only point where a god might be interjected into the cosmological evolution of the universe might be at the spark that set off the "big bang". Perhaps a god set off that spark, but the principles of quantum mechanics can explain the origin of the "big bang" without the need for a god. Accordingly, the universe and its continued existence was not created by a god, but by naturally occurring physical phenomena.

If a god didn't create the universe, how did it evolve? We know that it began with the "big bang" and continuously evolved from there. As a slight sidetrack, I purposely use the words "evolved" and "evolution" because they should be the most important words in the human vocabulary. I know, the words "evolution" and "evolved" sometimes provoke fear and blasphemy in humans, but they should be words endeared by humans. Without evolution, humans as we know them, would not have come into existence. Evolution really tells us that everything will change with time, things are changing at this very moment and will continue to change into the future, and this is what the word "evolution" tells us. Life has the ability to adapt to changes, so evolution has been good for life. The entire universe has undergone continuous changes since its inception. At first subatomic particles crystallized out of a very hot plasma that consisted of electrons and smaller subatomic particles that would condense into protons and neutrons which in turn would condense into atoms of hydrogen. Gravitational attraction between the atoms of hydrogen would condense into giant spheres that would capture more atoms, when these became sufficiently large, the gravitational pressure at the centers of these spheres would rip neutrons and protons from their locations in the nuclei of their respective atoms. This would release enough energy to ignite these spheres into hydrogen bomb infernos. The first stars would be born and this would bring light to the universe. These giant spheres would attract other gaseous spheres gravitationally and galaxies would come into existence. In the meantime the explosive forces of hydrogen blasts within the burning stars would constantly cast off their source of energy and become highly condensed neutron stars, which, if large enough, would explode into a supernova and form all the heavier elements that we know and use today. The universe continues to expand, new stars are constantly formed, and old stars return their contents to the universe for recycling. If a star, at its death, is really gigantic, it may collapse into a black hole and engulf all nearby matter including light. What happens to this matter? No one really knows, perhaps it becomes "dark matter" and "dark energy", or perhaps, as the math suggests, it collapses into a singularity and becomes nothing. The universe has a dynamic position, it is constantly changing or constantly evolving.

Like the universe, the planet Earth is constantly evolving. After our Sun amassed sufficient hydrogen atoms to compress its interior to the point that it became so hot that protons and neutrons burst from their bonds in nuclei and ignited the hydrogen blasts that continue today and for billions of years into the future. At the time of ignition, the Sun must have been near its greatest mass and gravitationally attracted nearby gases, atoms from supernova explosions, meteors, asteroids, and comets that went into orbit around the Sun and eventually coalesced into the masses that constitute the planets of the Sun. The Sun continued to attract meteors, asteroids, and comets so the planets were bombarded by these objects, and heat from the Sun for almost a billion years after the Sun ignited. During this time the Sun lost some of its mass, cooled a bit, and swept most of the objects from around its orbit, so the planets were no longer bombarded by a plethora of objects and they cooled to more solidified form. At first, our planet Earth had no atmosphere, so it had no protection from the Sun's radiation and remained hot. Gases from the hot Earth escaped into the atmosphere and as the Earth grew in mass from bombarding meteors, it became large enough to hold molecules within its gravitational grasp and slowly developed an atmosphere. The acquisition of an atmosphere blocked radiation from the Sun and permitted the Earth to cool over the next several hundred thousand years. As the Earth cooled, moisture in the atmosphere and from bombarding comets condensed into water and the great oceans on Earth came into existence. Water diluted salts on the surface of Earth and brought an ingredient essential to life as we know it. The Earth cooled to the point that life could come into existence and tiny bacteria like creatures appeared. These creatures changed through billions of years and changed with the changes that took place on the surface of Earth and in the oceans. The genetic material, the DNA, in tiny bacteria like creatures, the first organisms to live on planet Earth, changed with the many changes that took place on Earth, eventually gave rise to all the plants and animals that existed through all of time and to humans as we know them today.

TRACKING HUMAN ORIGINS

In reality, the origin of humans should go back to the first DNA molecules to survive the turmoils of Earth's early environment. If this were not the case, humans would not be present on Earth today. This precludes the possibility that humans were created by a god as many humans believe to this day, so we have to ask: Were humans created by a god or were humans created by humans through a naturally occurring procreational evolutionary process just like the cosmological universe and the Earth itself? From the outset, evolution is and has always been a part of the history of the universe, our Sun and our Earth. Evolution of the Sun, the Earth, and all the plants and animals on the Earth is fact, a law, not theory. The cosmological development of the Sun and Earth are known. The development of the plants and animals on Earth is traceable to previously existing plants and animals, not to creations by a god. It is not possible to trace human DNA back to the original DNA that survived through the ages. The quantities of DNA have increased tremendously, and many new DNA sequences have come into existence to account for the tremendous number of new proteins for each new species that has come into existence. New DNA sequences were essential to account for the great diversity of life that has existed on Earth over billions of years, so I shall limit this discussion to the origin of humans from their hominid ancestors. The fossil records of bones and teeth traces humans, as we know them today, back some six million years to _Orrorin tugenensis_, found in Africa, a hominid lived in trees and on the ground, and so far, evidence from CAT scans of a femur makes this fossil species the first with the ability to consistently walk upright as humans today. At the present time Orrorin could very well represent the first hominid with the genetic information that could give rise to humans. The discoverers of Orrorin give that species a fairly direct ancestry to _Homo ergaster_. A species of hominid that appeared in Africa at a much later time, but they have Orrorin on a direct line to Ergaster who developed into _Homo heidelbergensis_. Heidelbergensis in turn gave rise to modern humans in Africa and neandertals in Europe and the Middle East with all other hominids as side branches and that includes all the australopithicenes. The next hominid to make an appearance on Earth was _Ardipithecus_ *ramidus*. Ardipithecus was found in Ethiopia and entered the picture about one and a half million years after Orrorin, so Orrorin could be ancestral to Ardipithicus, but this has not been suggested. On the other hand, fossils of Ardipithecus have definite hominid features that place it on a direct evolutionary line to the australopithicenes. In particular to <u>Australopithecus anamensis</u>, this species appeared in Kenya more than four million years ago and appears to be the species that gave rise to <u>Australopithecus afarensis</u>. Several species of Australopithecus appeared in Africa at the same time, but evidence from Afarensis places this species on the evolutionary line that led to modern humans. Other species of Australopithecus gave rise to other species that continued the Australopithecus line up to a rather short time ago, three hundred thousand years, but the fossil evidence indicates that these species were not in line with the genetic path to modern humans.

Most paleoanthropologists are in agreement that Afarensis was ancestral to <u>Homo habilis</u>, a large group of fossils that place it on the direct line to humans with the retention of some Australopithecus features. Habilis appeared on the scene over two million years ago. Fossils of Habilis have only been found in Africa along with a large cache of stone tools, so Habilis, with its expanded brain case and knowledge of how to make stone tools gave the appearance that it was definitely making a contribution to the survival of a species that could be ancestral to modern humans, and most paleoanthropologists place <u>Homo habilis</u>, with its stone tools, as a central figure in the development of humans.

The extensive invasion of <u>Homo erectus</u> to lands distant from Africa certainly give this hominid vast adaptability which echoes the adaptive powers of humans today and places Erectus high on the list of candidates that developed into modern humans. The fossil record of Erectus indicates that the brain case had again expanded in size compared to that of _Homo habilis_. Erectus appears to be a direct descendant of Habilis but exhibits a more sophisticated set of stone tools, a very good possibility of fire control, and an expansive wanderlust. Numerous fossils of Erectus have been found in China, Indonesia, Europe, and The Republic of Georgia, current thought on Erectus travels have taken them from Africa to the Middle East where they spread into China and down to Indonesia and probably from Georgia into Europe. Certainly, they were superstars when it came to traversing the earth. Some paleoanthropologists believe that the Erectus in China gave rise to the Chinese, the Erectus (Heidelbergensis) in Europe gave rise to the neandertals in Europe, the Erectus in the Middle East were ancestral to the neandertals found in the Middle East, and the Erectus in Africa were ancestral to humans in Africa.

At one time there appeared to be a fairly direct ancestral relationship from _Homo habilis_ to _Homo erectus_ to humans, _Homo sapiens_, but with the appearance of more fossil hominids this direct relationship no longer looked so direct and needed modification. Now four species seem to be in line as the direct ancestors to humans, _Homo erectus_, _Homo ergaster_, _Homo heidelbergensis_, and _Homo antecessor_. All three appear to be descendants of _Homo habilis_ but some paleoarcheologists say that Ergaster in Africa and Erectus are the same, so they make Erectus ancestral to Heidelbergensis who in turn was ancestral to both humans and neandertals. Others place Erectus as a branch that is not on the lineage to humans, and make Heidelbergensis a descendant of Ergaster with Heidelbergensis again giving rise to both humans and neandertals. Still others say that all three are Erectus, but they should remain as three different species because they have vastly different survival times, and they have been separated by long distances for long periods of time. Some Erectus survived out of Africa until ancient humans migrated out of Africa, but all Erectus surviving in places other than Africa appear to have become extinct. In addition, it is interesting to note that the neandertals met the same fate as Erectus but they continued to survive until after the arrival of ancient humans in Europe and the Middle East.

Some paleoanthropologists have given Erectus the distinction of giving rise to the neandertals, _Homo neandertalensis_, population in the Middle East and at a later time, to the neandertal population in Europe. This is in contrast to the consensus candidate giving Heidelbergensis the distinction of being ancestral to neandertals.

New hominid fossils, _Homo antecessor_, found in mountain sites in northern Spain offer a different lineage. The people working with Antecessor make _Homo ergaster_ in Africa ancestral to Antecessor in Africa. Antecessor moved out of Africa to the Middle East and to Europe about a million years ago. In Europe Antecessor developed into Heidelbergensis and on to neandertals. In Africa, the genome of Antecessor was altered to a new species of archaic human, _Homo sapiens_, the ancient humans who migrated out of Africa. Thus, they say that Antecessor is the link between humans and neandertals. In this scheme both _Homo erectus_ and _Homo heidelbergensis_ are not on the evolutionary line to humans.

It may seem a little confusing to have four candidates as the direct ancestors to humans but all have features that place them on the line to humans. As already pointed out, they might be the same species and this will be sorted out as more fossils appear. The important point, a continuum of fossils of human ancestors have been found in the earth of our planet Earth.

Genetic modifications and consequent adaptations to their survival circumstances must have brought *Homo erectus* or *Homo ergaster*, or *Homo heidelbergensis*, or *Homo antecessor*, the genetic basis for archaic humans, *Homo sapiens*, with an ever more expanded brain case and an even more sophisticated tool chest. Comparative studies of mitochondrial DNA, DNA from the Y-chromosome, and sequencing of amino acids in several biochemically vital proteins indicate that ancient humans expanded out of Africa around sixty thousand years ago and gave rise to the populations of humans present on Earth today. One last expansion of the brain and skull of *Homo sapiens* brought the arrival of modern humans, *Homo sapiens sapiens*, and their abilities to express themselves with small sculptures, and with sculptural reliefs and paintings on the walls of caves in France and Spain more than thirty-five thousand years ago.

This brief history of humans from six million years ago to the present could be extended farther back in time but the result would be the same. There has been no divine intervention in the development of humans over the six million years covered in this account. From the first humanoid to consistently walk on two feet to *Homo sapiens sapiens*, genetic modifications permitted adaptations to environments that changed over millions of years. These adaptations have been recorded in the fossil records and show a continuum of change to humans as they exist today. Humans didn't abruptly appear on the surface of Earth already conditioned and adapted to Earth's environment. Humans originated from previously existing humans. Over millions of generations new combinations of genes have led humans from individuals with very small brains and small skulls, individuals who could barely walk on two feet, to humans with very large brains and large skulls with signs of ever increasing brain power and the abilities to walk, run, and jump on only two feet. Supernatural gods did not create humans, humans gave rise to humans through the natural procreational process over many millions of years.

THE FIRST SIGNS OF SPIRITUAL THOUGHT

It doesn't appear that *Homo erectus* ever buried their dead, but there is evidence from the hominid sites in Spain that *Homo antecessor* may have buried some of their dead and the neandertals definitely buried their dead. The thought is that Antecessor spread out of Africa about one million years ago and made its appearance in Spain at least 780,000 years ago. In Europe, Antecessor developed into *Homo heidelbergensis* by around 600,000 years ago and Heidelbergensis gave rise to the neandertals around 300,000 years ago, and they survived to at least 30,000 years ago. If Antecessor buried their dead then the neandertal line in Europe had thoughts about burials for a long long time. The human line from Antecessor in Africa is not so clear, but the modern humans, *Homo sapiens sapiens*, who painted the caves in France and Spain 35,000 years ago, also buried their dead and must have had thoughts about burials. Burying their dead would indicate that they were thinking about the possibility that life might continue after death. If we take care of the body, the person within, the spirit, might continue after death. A life governed by the spirits of the dead with the possibility of a spiritual leader, a spirit who could be considered a god. Thus, human ancestors and neandertals invented the possibility of a life after death, they invented their spirits, and probably invented a spiritual personage who could be considered a spiritual leader, a god. This came at a time when humans first thoughtfully placed their dead into graves that they dug out of the earth, so humans and neandertals invented spirits and gods a long time ago, in the neighborhood of 100,0000 years and maybe 780,000 years ago. Ever since, the spirits and gods of humans have become more complex with the development of entire civilizations based on gods and spirits that first entered the brains of human and neandertal ancestors. Thus, the spirits and gods of humans have human origin many thousands of millenia ago, so thoughts of gods have been with the human brain for at least tens of thousands of years.

GOD AS THE COLLECTIVE THOUGHTS OF HUMANS

If humans invented their gods and gave them human characteristics, and humans came into existence from previously existing humans and their ancestors, and humans who could write wrote the words of human gods, then humans must be the god or gods that humans know. If humans are the god of humans, how might that work? Many millennia ago when humans were first inventing thoughts of their gods and a world of life after death, and when they first started burying their dead, they would meet other humans in the course of their daily activities. They would discuss their thoughts on gods, spirits, life after death, and burials. At times they would find that some humans had the same thoughts while others were hearing about these subjects for the first time. Soon, those who had never thought about gods, spirits, life after death, and burials were thinking about those subjects. These humans would then discuss their thoughts with other humans and before long an entire population of humans over a large area were finding that the humans in that population were thinking about gods, spirits, life after death, and burials, and they were in agreement with the thoughts of other humans in that area, and they were all burying their dead with objects that were used in life. This would have been the first collection of humans who were thinking collectively and were in basic agreement about their thoughts on gods, spirits, life after death, and burial, and they may have chosen a supreme leader. This would have been the first god designated by the collective thoughts of the humans who were in agreement on the subjects of gods, spirits, life after death, and burials.

Collective thoughts such as this were not confined to one area of the world. Humans in distant lands started to bury their dead without the knowledge that humans in other parts of the world were burying their dead. The collective thoughts of the ancient cultures of Egypt, Mesoamerica, and Mesopotamia are examples of humans coming together to build monuments to their thoughts on life after death, pyramids, temples and caves for Egypt and Mesoamerica, and ziggurats for Mesopotamia. Building these monuments was not a one time thing, they continued to build these structures over thousands of years to satisfy their thoughts on their gods, spirits, and the world of life after death. The collective thoughts of the humans building these monuments must have been passed from generation to generation because the structures and what they were used for lasted not for just a hundred years but for thousands.

In the world today, large numbers, millions to billions, of humans constitute the major religions of the world. Each religion has rules, beliefs, personages, history, philosophy, and words that are characteristic of a particular religion. Each of these religions may have millions of humans who believe and follow the teachings of a particular religion. These millions of people will all have the same beliefs and thoughts on their particular religion. This would constitute the collective thought of millions of people on the same subject. The collective thought of these masses would be uniform for their religion and would have the power of the collective thought of millions of humans. This would be the power of god witnessed by millions with exactly the same thoughts, so the collective thoughts of large masses of humans would be god in action.

We had a very recent example of the uniform power of collective thought. Pope John Paul II died. Millions of people with the same collective thoughts descended on Rome to witness the funeral of John Paul. Rome was not turned into a city of chaos, the collective thoughts of millions from around the world maintained order and civility, a few suffered from dehydration, and many waited for hours, but the collective thoughts were focused on getting everyone through the public ceremony in a reverent and healthy fashion. The collective thoughts of millions of humans were again called into action for the election of a new pope, Pope Benedict XVI. Again, millions gathered in Rome with only minor incidents. Thus, the collective thoughts of masses of humans could be the gods of humans, and definitely represent human thought in a benevolent democratic society.

EPILOGUE

Early contact with the christian religion led me to believe that their god was a supernatural superior spirit who was ordained with the form and characteristics of humans, so I pictured god as a ghostly spirit who had the appearance of a strong and often forceful human, a god with very human features. Over the years this picture was reinforced by pictures that I saw at church, by pictures displayed by friends and relatives, and by movies that I attended. This picture gave me a definite association with this god, I was human and the christian god had features similar to mine. When I went to university I found that there was more than one god. This was confusing at first because I had been led to believe that there was and should be only one god, the christian god that I knew in my more youthful days. After a period of confusion, I began a quest to look into the major religions of the world to find the nature of the gods of these religions. I found that all the gods of religious orders and the gods of ancient civilizations were ordained with different characteristics but all gave their gods human features of one sort or another. Furthermore, all religions, including those that do not appear to have gods, Yoga and Transcendental Meditation, expressed a form of life after death. Even the gods and spirits of ancient civilizations were designed to assist people in their life after death, and this was undoubtedly in the thoughts of the humans who first buried their dead long ago. A life after death is a common principle that all humans through all times would embrace, the human brain would issue forth with thought, what an excellent idea, I wouldn't have to die at the time of my death, I could live on in a life after death, religions give me this opportunity. Unfortunately, there is one masterful flaw with this thought, as pointed out in Chapter 3, this thought can only continue in a living thinking brain, when the brain dies thought dies, when thought dies so goes the thought of a life after death, but then, if the brain is dead, it matters not, no more problems to solve.

This seems to leave humans without hope of a life after death, if this thought, that has been with humans since they started burying their dead, vanishes with the death of the brain, where do humans turn for advancement of their thoughts? As indicated, the universe and Earth, as well as humans, continue to evolve. The human brain has evolved from the size of a small ape like hominid to almost fifteen hundred cubic centimeters for the brain of modern humans. In this time human thought has gone from day to day survival to thoughts about the origin and fate of the universe and humans in an ever expanding cosmos. Human thought has evolved with the human brain and there is absolutely every reason to predict that human thought will continue to evolve and solve ever more complex problems. Human evolution must eventually come to the point where humans realize and recognize that the gods of humans are humans. Humans have given their characteristics and thoughts to the gods that they have invented. Human gods exist in the thoughts of humans so that makes human gods the property of human thought. Human thought is the property of the human brain, the human brain arose from prior human brains, this would make the gods of human thought humans with human brains and the ability to think about gods. Therefore, the gods of human thought originate in the human brain, so the gods of humans have origin in humans, so the gods of humans are humans. That makes me a god and you a god and all humans, who exist now and in the past, gods and humans, with the ability to think up gods who will serve the thoughts of humans.

More than likely, the collective thoughts of masses of humans could very well be the gods of humans, they support and agree on the same subject matters, or is that theocracy or democracy in action?

Chapter 3

LIFE AFTER DEATH

DOES LIFE CONTINUE AFTER DEATH?

The first indication that humans began to think that there might be a continuation of life after death came when they began to bury their dead with objects that were used, worn, or cherished during their life. According to the archeological record this practice began almost one hundred thousand years ago when humans began to collect brightly colored rocks, make necklaces, and paint themselves with colored powders. Some of these rocks and powders, and a few other objects, that may have been used in life, have been found in paleolithic burials. For what reason would objects that were collected and used by living humans begin to appear in burials? It could have been as a simple sentimental gesture, or the persons conducting the burial knew that the objects were special to the dead person and thought that they should be included, or the dead individual may have been a chief or a shaman so objects that indicated their high status were included in the burial out of respect for the individual, or the thought may have been: There may be a possibility that life might continue after death. This person used these objects while living, perhaps if we include these objects with the burial, the dead person may be able to use these objects while enjoying some form that resembled life before death even though the body of the person was lifeless. Burying personal objects with the body of the dead would be a definite indication that humans were beginning to think that there may be a form of life after death. So the thought of life after death has been in the human mind for a long time and once sparked must have been passed from one generation to the next.

The thought that there might be a form of life after death must have persisted through the millennia to a time some thirty-five thousand years ago when modern humans with enlarged brains carried the life after death theme to the walls of caves in France and Spain. Certainly, the effort that was put into those cave paintings would suggest that they were more than pictures of animals and in instances, how they were killed. The paintings must have been to honor the animals that sustained the lives of the people living at the time. They must have known that the paintings would not disappear in a short period of time since the paintings would be in place on the cave walls when they returned to paint a new animal or scene. The thought must have arisen that the paintings would live on after the death of the animals, after the deaths of the person or persons who killed the animals, and after the deaths of the persons who painted depictions of the animals on the cave walls. This tells us that the people thought that the animals had a spiritual existence that persisted after death, and they were painting the spirit that lived on after the animal had been killed because the painting lived on after the animal had been killed. At the same time, the humans making the paintings must have thought that they had a spirit that lived after their death. If the animals had a spirit that lived on after death, the humans must have thought they had a spirit that lived after death. What makes the thoughts of spiritual beings more significant is the extent to which they continued to be painted, from thirty-five thousand years ago to twelve thousand years ago, not just a few hundred years but thousands.

As time progressed the idea of a form of life after death must have became further entrenched in the minds of people who were developing the first known civilizations, the people in China, Mesopotamia, and Egypt. Even before five thousand years ago burials in these areas were being elaborately stocked with items that were used by the living. Again indicating that people were thinking that life didn't stop at death, it continued on in another form that could use and gain comfort from objects that were used while people were living.

LIFE AFTER DEATH CONTINUES IN SPIRITUAL FORM?

So, the theme of life after death is not a recent human acquisition but must have been in the thoughts of the humans who first included objects with burials. With time that theme gained momentum and by this time may have become part of the human genome. Egyptian thought was embedded with the idea of life after death, an "afterlife" that continued in the "underworld". The greeks came along with gods that had spiritual form that could influence the physical world. The romans took over the gods of the greeks, so they too had ideas of a spiritual world. As an entirely isolated development, the mayan people in Mesoamerica developed a spiritual world that lived above the earth, a middle world for humans, and an underworld with spirits that had entrance to the physical world through caves. Even the "ball games" of the mayan people were spiritual in nature with the losing team serving as sacrifice with honor because the sacrificed players would enter the spiritual world as envisioned by the mayans. All modern religious orders are based on the very ancient thought of a life after death and have embraced the theme of a spirit that can leave the body after death and live in a spiritual world. Thus, human thoughts on life after death have continuity, they have been in existence in the human mind since humans first started to bury objects with the bodies of the dead. Through all the millennia since that time, thoughts of a life after death have been continuously present in the human mind thus giving a continuity of thought through the ages.

The egyptians went on to define forms of life after death. They didn't explicitly refer to their forms as spirits, more like forces that gave a person life, but with recent thought and language we would refer to these as spirits. The ancient egyptians had three spirits, the Ka, the Ba, and the Akh. The Ka force came into existence at birth, stayed with the body through life and parted to the underworld at the death of the individual. The Ba spirit required a body, hence, the development of elaborate procedures to preserve the body after death. The Ba spirit was more like a modern definition of personality. It was free to travel from the physical body in a tomb to the underworld and supposedly to other parts of the world but had to return to the body every night or the physical body would not survive, hence, the development of elaborate means to preserve the body. The Ba spirit had to have union with a physical body and provided it with food and pleasure. The Akh spirit was the form that survived forever in the underworld, but the Akh spirit depended on the union of Ba and Ka spirits in the underworld. The egyptians carried the idea of spirits even further, pharaohs were endowed with the spirit of Ra, the sun god, with that spirit the pharaoh became a god and had to be treated as a living god in life and in death, so the spirits of the pharaohs lived on after their deaths and the burials became extremely elaborate with items suitable for the rule of pharaohs as gods and as pharaohs after their deaths.

LIFE AFTER DEATH: A POWERFUL THOUGHT

The spiritual themes of the ancient egyptians incorporated a living spirit into the physical body, and endowed that spirit with the ability to survive death, leave the body, and perpetuate a spiritual form of life after death. This theme had vast power: A living spirit was present in the live physical body, a spirit that had the ability to leave the body at death and perpetuate a spiritual form of life after death, once born, a person never died. Who could resist the power of such thought. Especially humans who had no knowledge of physics, chemistry, or biology at the time. People from the area surrounding Egypt must have seen the monuments, buildings, sculptures and hieroglyphic writings that were devoted to the egyptian idea of spirit and life after death. Certainly, they would have been impressed and influenced by the immensity of those works and the spiritual ideas that they conveyed.

Humans in parts of the world other than Egypt, Mesopotamia, China, and Mesoamerica also included objects from life in their burials, and must have had thoughts on a form of life after death. Possibly, an idea similar to the egyptian's "Ka", a spiritual form that had the capacity to leave the body when death arrived. An impressive thought that must have been the subject of tales told to people in distant lands. Such a theme would have great appeal to most living humans, think, humans don't die when life passes from their body, they live on as a spirit in the spiritual world. The spiritual themes of the ancient egyptians must have influenced many people in that part of the world, and, over time, led them to incorporate similar themes into their developing religious thoughts.

The ancient egyptians also had a measure of life that gained perpetuity. The egyptians took the heart as the seat of the soul/spirit during life. At death, they believed that the spiritual deeds of the heart were weighed against a spiritual feather. If the balance tipped to the heart, then that person was not permitted to enter the spiritual world of life after death, however, if the balance tipped to the feather, then that person was permitted to enter the world of life after death. In most instances the feather outweighed the heart. This was another idea that influenced thought in that part of the world. It appears very much like the measure of good deeds against bad. Some religions point to a heaven and a hell, if you have been good in life and obey the teachings of your special religious order then your spirit will pass judgment and it will reside in heaven, but if you have not been good in life and have not obeyed the teachings of your religious order, then your spirit will not pass judgment and it will be banished to a place known as hell. These thoughts are very similar to the egyptian weighing of the heart and point to an egyptian influence on developing religious orders.

THE FORM OF THE HUMAN SPIRIT

If every human body has a living spirit that has the ability to leave the body at the time of its death, what form does the spirit take after it leaves the body?

Humans seem to think of their spirits as having human form, a form that is totally without physical matter, a diaphenous ether that exists between the atoms and molecules of space. These ethereal spirits have been with human thought for thousands of millennia, so these thoughts should not be taken lightly, and over the millenna have developed persistent and perhaps genetic characteristics. Humans visualize a spirit residing within the human body. That spirit remains with the body throughout life, but leaves the body at the time of death to assume an ethereal form. The ethereal form retains all the attributes that an individual possessed while living, so the individual spirit will continue a humanistic existence after leaving the physical body. In life the brain gives the ability to think, to store information, to recall specific information at will and use that information in thought, to correlate information with thought and thought with stored information. The brain uses immediately perceived information and information that has been stored for many many years. When humans think or visualize a spirit they give that spirit all of the thoughts and all of the information that was present in the brain at the time of death. Humans in general visualize the intact passage of all thoughts and stored information to the spirit as it leaves the body, thus giving the spirit the ability to think and visualize and use the stored information in exactly the same manner as the living brain. This is the form that human thought gives to human spirits, and as thought, the spirit is given the physical characteristics of the individual as last experienced in the living state, but the form retains an ethereal mystical existence.

RELIGIONS EXPOUND THE HUMANISTIC APPROACH

The teachings of most religions, both present and past, tell their followers that there is a form of life after death. Like the ancient egyptians, the spirit or soul of modern religions has the ability to leave the body after its physical life has been declared mentally nonfunctional and its heart has stopped beating so that oxygenated blood no longer circulates to the tissues of the body to keep them in a viable state. After this point the spirit has the ability to leave the body and engage in activities similar to those that it encountered while living, but the activities take on a more ethereal state. Religions naturally rallied around a theme of life after death and must have been automatically ordained to think that a spirit that lived after death would be a more humanistic approach to death than the thought that the dead body would just lay in the cold ground doing nothing.

Is it no wonder that modern religious philosophies have incorporated these very ancient thoughts of spirits into their philosophies. They have given spirits the ability to leave the physical body on death and continue life as spirits. The people back in the days when most modern religions came into existence knew very little about the physical-chemical-biological world, and practically nothing about how the body functioned. In their minds they brought forth gods and spirits of the past, and gods and spirits of unknown origin to explain phenomena for which they had no explanation. Over the millennias of their existence in the human brain, these spirits have become thoroughly embedded in human minds, and so their existence has appeared in the thoughts of humans over every part of the world, and incorporated into all religious philosophies that spread the word that all humans should believe in their gods and spirits that live in a world of life after death.

All the religions that I have encountered in my studies; Christian, Hindu, Celtic, Islam, Jewish, Buddhist, Confucius, Sikh, Yoga, mythologies of ancient Egypt and Mesopotamia, and the spirituality of the indigenous peoples of Australia and Africa; mostly from art history, express some form of life after death even though the ways of achieving life after death differ.

I think that I know one religion that does not express the idea of a spiritual form of life after death. The Shinto religion in Japan finds beauty in the natural placement and juxtaposition of objects found in nature. These are special places that are held in reverence as nature's gifts to the viewer and may be spiritual but not in the sense that the natural setting under view has a spirit that will live after death. However, upon review, the person viewing the natural setting would no doubt know that the setting will continue long after the death of the viewer, so in a sense this would be a form of life after death to the person viewing the setting, but in this case a spirit that leaves the body after death would not be involved. Viewing these special sites in nature would probably enhance the pleasure sites of the viewer, and the viewer may think that these special places in nature were put together by some power beyond the power of humans but a power of nature, not a power conceived in the human mind.

HUMAN SPIRITS PICTURED WITH HUMAN SHAPE

The visualization of human spirits by most present day humans has been influenced by artistic depictions of the gods, the spirits of gods, and the spirits of religious figures. The writers, painters and sculptors of ancient Egypt pictured their gods and spirits with animal features but with human bodies, so their thoughts on human spirits were undoubtedly pictured in the mind as human. The sculptors of the Olmecs and Mayans from ancient Mesoamerica depicted their gods with human form. For the christian world visualization of christian religious figures goes back to the gothic period and reaches the heights of artistic presentation in both painting and sculpture in the renaissance, the fourteen and fifteen hundreds. Most people living in christian countries today visualize human spirits as portrayed in the paintings of the renaissance, namely, as humans. Not unusual because Jesus was human, but his father was theoretically a god, so if the son of a god had human form, then the father must have some semblance to humans. People of the jewish faith visualize their god in human form. Artists, who depicted the buddhist god and religious personages associated with Buddha, have given these figures human characteristics, but then, Buddha was human, so the people devoted to Buddha no doubt visualize their spirits as taking on human form. Sculptors and artists from ancient India have given their gods human form. It is apparent that artists spread over the entire world have pictured the gods and spiritual figures with human form. Over the years many billions of people have seen these artistic expressions of gods and spirits. These expressions have undoubtedly influenced how people think of their gods and spirits, namely, they think of them with human form and human characteristics, but often with very special features that are represented in the works of art. Humans recognize the special features and that brings them to understand the relationships that humans have given to their gods, spirits, and religious figures.

THE POWER OF THE BRAIN

If the spirit has the ability to leave the body after death, what retains the spirit within the body while it is in the living state? The answer is very direct and very simple: The spirit does not have the ability to leave the body, so it never leaves the body! However, the practioners of many disciplines would have us believe otherwise. This includes all the humans who believe that a spirit leaves the body at the time of death, and would also include humans who hold the views of the practioners of yoga, and those who believe in transcendental meditation and the cosmic conscience. Their ultimate goal is to enter a state wherein the mind transcends the physical body, enters into an ethereal state that permits the mind with all of its knowledge to travel the world at ethereal time, in ethereal space, and either gain knowledge or exert influence in a spiritual manner. In this way the mind can gain knowledge that it would not normally access, or gain knowledge that would otherwise take time beyond belief. During this time, the mind can become endowed with wisdom that can be put to use upon the mind's return to the physical body. In this instance the mind could be the spirit, so practitioners of deep meditative states might believe that the mind/spirit has the ability to leave the body and return when they return to a conscious state, but again, this endows the transcendental form with the ability to carry on with the functions of the brain as they exist in the living body, but does a transcendental form have a brain that can function as a normal human brain?

Does the mind/spirit actually transcend the body while in a deep meditative state? The person in a meditative trance may look upon the experience as an instance in which it appeared as if the mind/spirit left the body to travel willfully to distant places and return to the body once again. More than likely the mind made it appear as if it left the body and this was the impression that was given by the brain, but in reality the mind remained in association with its living brain. The living brain puts thoughts together and humans interpret these thoughts as a mind, the mind in turn tells the brain that it has conceived a form that can leave the body, a spiritual form of the mind that can leave the brain and return. After considerable meditation, the brain in turn puts this to a test of its abilities. It gives the mind the ability to conceive a spirit that it thinks has the ability to transcend its own brain and wander into unknown space, and the mind actually believes that it has achieved this instruction without giving credit to the brain so the brain has actually tricked the mind into believing that it has sent a spiritual entity out of the body, a spiritual entity that the brain returns to the mind making it think that it has been on an important mission or journey, and the brain has done all of this within its own boundaries. Thus, illustrating that the brain is a very powerful instrument.

THE BRAIN, THE MIND, AND THE SPIRIT

This brings up the interdependence of the brain, the mind, and the spirit/soul. What is the relationship between the brain, the mind, and the spirit? The living naturally functional human brain is the source of all human thought and thought gives rise to the mind but the mind encompasses all thought and more. The mind is the totality of the brain, which means the brain gives the ability to think, to store information, to recall specific information at will and use that information in thought, and to correlate information with thought and use thought to recall and correlate stored information. The living brain has the ability to store thoughts, and sensory and perceived information for very long periods of time. The living brain has the ability to use its stored information for immediate reaction to its environment and to encounters with other humans. These abilities of the brain give rise to the mind, the totality of the brain. If the mind is the totality of the brain with all the abilities that encompass the brain then the spirit, as conceived by the brain, must also represent the totality of the brain with all of its abilities, so the mind and the spirit have the same identity and would be synonymous, but humans, in thought, give the spirit a separate identity that has the ability to leave the body at the time of death, but this may occur only in the thoughts of humans, so the spirit and the mind are most likely synonymous. Thus, the mind has origin in a fully functional brain, and the spirit originates as a conception of the brain, so mind and spirit are totally dependent on a living brain.

THE HUMAN BRAIN SUPERCEDES THE SPIRIT

Life after death is neither physically nor physiologically possible. The spirit would have to have the ability to function as the brain with thought, with the ability to store information and use stored information, with the ability of sensory detection and the ability to react to sensory detection, and with the ability to formulate speech and understand speech. Does a spiritual form of life have these capabilities? Yes it does, but only in the minds of humans. Human minds give the spirit that lives on after death the same abilities that the physical body and brain had in life, but this capacity is only a visualization that is given to the spirit by the capabilities of the human brain. Spirits are not physical entities with living functional brains. Without living human brains to give spirits the ability to function as living brains, spirits must remain as entities or thoughts brought into existence by the brains of living humans. So, in reality, it is not possible for spirits, who have separated from the human body and brain to have the capabilities of a human brain.

Without a physical physiologically functional brain, it would be impossible for any spirit to function as a human with an intact functional brain. How can a spirit function as a human? It can't. Spirits are only entities of the human brain and only live as thoughts in the human mind which gives spirits the attributes to carry on as living humans in the spiritual world, but spirits only live as thoughts in the brain, they are not physical entities. When the brain dies it is no longer capable of thought. The presence of a mind is dependent on a fully functional brain, a dead brain is no longer empowered with thought, therefore, when the brain dies the mind dies. The spirit, like the mind, is a conception of the brain, so it must die when the brain dies. Thus, the spirit can only be present in a body with a live fully functional brain because the spirit exists in the brain as thought, so the spirit cannot leave a dead body because the brain would be dead and incapable of thought so the spirit would pass out of existence at the time the brain dies.

If spirits are entities of thought and thought is a function of the brain, is it possible to separate thought from the brain, to project thought into space as a functional spirit? I would have to say that this too is an impossibility. The brain functions and thought arises in the brain, but without a functional brain thought would not exist, so the existence of thought without a brain would not be possible. However, the human brain is an extremely powerful entity and can conjure phenomena to its liking if given the opportunity. The brain in all of its power can and does influence matters at hand and those that may seem at great distance, but thought and the mind, as a totality of the brain, cannot function without a living brain. When the brain dies, thought dies; when thought dies, the mind dies; when the mind dies, the spirit dies.

SUMMARY

Spirits and gods have existed in the human mind for many millennia, the existence of spirits and gods in the mind for such a lengthy period has given their existence almost universal approval, and almost absolute belief in their existence as entities that transcend human thought. Over the millennia humans have come to believe that the gods and spirits of the mind have an existence that has separated from the human body, mind, and brain. Humans have given these gods and spirits the ability to live after the death of the body, and the ability to think and act like humans as they existed in life. They have often endowed their gods and spirits with abilities far beyond the human experience, they have been given superhuman power to raise them above human thought and beyond the abilities of the brain, but their origin stems from human thought. The creation of human gods and spiritual worlds to alleviate thoughts of great loss at the time of death is certainly an admirable quality put forth by the brain to relieve mental anguish over the loss of humans known and loved in life. The human brain found a way to ease the mental pain of death and invented gods and spirits that would not die at death but would live on in a spirit world overseen by gods. However, can a spirit exist in the absence of the brain that gave it existence? Spirits and gods are not physical physiological entities with living brains. They do not have the powers of the brain and only exist as thoughts in the living functional brain. Humans have encompassed the thought of life after death because humans don't cherish the thought that life will end at the time of death, so they gladly extend life beyond death, in a spiritual world created in the thoughts of a living brain. Without a human brain it would be impossible for spirits and gods to exist and function outside of the human body.

Be assured, though, humans live on after death, they live indelibly in the minds of the people with whom they had contact, their friends and acquaintances, in the minds of the humans who loved them, in the minds of the humans they loved, even in the minds of enemies.

Chapter 4

ELIMINATING TERRORISM

HUMAN BOMBS

The most devastating human activity makes use of humans to serve as mobile bombs, a drastically extreme form of terrorism. These human bombs attach numerous sticks of dynamite to their bodies and camouflage the dynamite by covering it with clothing. Thus, they appear just as any other person who may be shopping, walking, looking, driving, riding a bus, or going to school, work, or church, and this is what makes human bombs so devastating as a terrorist tactic. Human bombs are very hard to detect, they can mingle right in with human targets, and they not only eliminate themselves when they detonate but they kill and wound many persons in their immediate surroundings, which is their purpose, of course. There is another form of human bomb that can be more devastating, namely, the drivers of cars, vans and trucks that have been loaded with tons of dynamite and purposely driven into buildings, convoys, and large gatherings of people. These can also be very effective terrorist devices, but they are much more expensive and defenses can be put in place to deter these human driven bombs. Nevertheless, they can be very accurate and destructive. These human bombs make very effective terrorist weapons and are my concern here.

UNDERSTANDING HUMAN BOMBS

In order to understand how we might eliminate human bombs, we should look into their origin. Where do the humans who are very willing to sacrifice their material bodies in a self-induced explosion, originate? They are frequently younger members of very religious families. From birth they have been taught that their materialistic body is a form in which they will spend a brief time on Earth. Their spiritual form will continue on forever after they have died. This spiritual form is the important form for the continuation of life after death, a comforting thought in itself. They have been instructed by clerics, elders, friends, peers, and relatives that their life will continue in a world without disease, in a world with a bountiful supply of the most desired foods, a world in which love abounds and sexual desires are always fulfilled, a world in which anger, killing, and war are unknown, a world in which death and ageing do not exist. If you serve as a human bomb and fulfill your assigned task, you and your family will be honored and receive special compensation in the world of life after death. Such is the beauty that you will receive, after you have completed the instructions that we have given at the appointed time and place. With the promise of such a bountiful life after death, who could refuse such an offer? Especially people who have never had an opportunity to approach a life of luxury and with little hope for such a life in the future.

The humans who serve as human bombs seem to be people who are susceptible to influence by clergy, elders, peers, friends, and relatives. Who would be more susceptible than those who have very little to begin with and of course children raised by the people of influence? (Susceptible humans would include martyrs because they would be readily susceptible to influence for a cause.) When the children reached adulthood they would be fully prepared for sacrifice as human bombs, and would consider their sacrifice a great honor to their families and to their influential acquaintances. Furthermore, they would have developed in an atmosphere that would have them believe that their lives on Earth would continue in a more bountiful form after their death, so death should not be feared but welcomed as the way to a much more magnificent form of life after death. Thus, human bombs would be fearless people who are thoroughly convinced that they will pass to a more beautiful life after their death, and this would be a certainty if they serve a cause and carry out their faith as a human bomb.

THE PEOPLE OF INFLUENCE

According to this, it would be futile to look to the human bombs themselves as a way to eliminate human bombs, but we should seriously consider the people who influence people to become human bombs. The people of influence, the clergy, elders, peers, friends, and relatives, direct the lives of their fellow humans so that they develop a desire to become human bombs if called upon to do so. Their direction comes from their thoughts and firm belief in religious teachings and studies of the correct way to fashion their lives after their religious leader who lives in their world of life after death. The great influence of the people of influence stems from their thoughts on the world of life after death, and their knowledge of the world of life after death. The knowledge of the present day people of influence has been influenced by people of influence and those people have been influenced by people of influence, and this goes on for generations. The result is an unfaltering belief in a world of life after death and their thoughts on such a world. Even though the humans who influence death dealing decisions have never been to or returned from their mythological world of life after death, a world that they have not personally experienced, a world that exists only in human thought. Yet, these clergy, elders, peers, friends and relatives can readily convince fellow humans that they should become human bombs and achieve a life after death by attaching dynamite to their bodies, or driving dynamite laden vehicles and killing themselves and others by exploding the dynamite. In order to achieve their goal of entrance into the world of life after death, the explosion must take place at a destination designated, most likely, by the persons who convinced the human bombers that their wishes for entrance into the world of life after death would only be granted after they had killed themselves and the maximum number of people in their immediate vicinity.

STRONG CONVICTIONS

Would it be possible to alter the thoughts of potential human bombs and convince them that there is no such world as the world of life after death? It is extremely doubtful that it would be possible to alter the thoughts of humans with the strong beliefs and convictions of human bombs. Even after knowledge of what they were going to do, what they would be required to do, and how they were going to kill themselves and many others, human bombers continue to carry out their missions. Humans, who have been thoroughly convinced and who very strongly believe that life in some form or another will continue after death, would find it impossible to alter their thoughts and conclude that there is no such world as the world of life after death. Thus, after generations of influence it would be extremely difficult to alter the thoughts of the people of influence so that they would influence the developing generation to believe that a world of life after death did not exist.

Such strong beliefs are undoubtedly planted in the brains of human bombs even as they grew during childhood, so the parties responsible for the deaths of human bombs and all their victims would have to be the clergy, elders, peers, friends, and relatives with whom they developed in life. It would be these people who planted the ideas of a bountiful life after death in the brains of humans who would become human bombs and it would be those people who should be responsible for the deaths of the human bombs and their victims, and those people would be the people of influence.

A PARADOX: TIME AND THOUGHT AND DEATH

If humans have been very strongly influenced to believe in life after death, then to those persons a form of life after death will exist in their thoughts right up and into the time of their death, and this brings out a paradox on human thought, death, and a world of life after death. It is this paradox that makes it extremely difficult to alter the thoughts of humans who strongly believe in a world of life after death. As a preamble to the paradox, human thought will continue in the human brain as long as the brain is functional, namely, right up to and into the point of death. At that time the brain is no longer functional, so thought is no longer possible. The paradox: Human bombs would go into death with thoughts that they would be going into the world of life after death, so their last thoughts before their brain becomes nonfunctional would be on their bountious life after death, so they would think that they were entering the world of life after death as their brain became nonfunctional and thoughtless, so for all practical purposes they would be entering the world of life after death as they died, and they would think that they were entering the world of life after death, but when thought was no longer possible the world of life after death would no longer exist in the brain of the dead individual, so in reality they would not enter the world of life after death and would die with the death of their brain.

Thoughts of an everlasting life would be present in the brain right up to the point of death so those humans would pass into death believing that they would pass into the form of life after death that they had been told to envision by the people of influence, so they will only know the thoughts of their living brain right up to the point of death and that would be about their wondrous life after their death, but that life would no longer exist after their death.

This brings in another question that requires an answer. What happens after the point of death? As we learned in the last chapter, when the brain dies, thought dies, a world of life after death exists in thoughts from a functional brain, so thoughts of a life after death would die, dead humans no longer have thoughts and would no longer have a life after death. Life after death has origin in human thought, human thought originates in the human brain, human thought can only arise in a living human brain, a living human brain can only exist in a living human, therefore, thoughts of life after death can only exist in a living human, so humans cannot live in a life after death, those thoughts must die with the death of the human brain.

PEOPLE OF INFLUENCE AND THE DEATH OF HUMAN BOMBS

However, this would no longer matter to dead humans, they would no longer have thoughts on their life or death. Their brains would be nonfunctional, so it would only be thoughts before death, that would be important to the lives of human bombs while their brains were still functional right up to the point of death. At the same time, the people of influence, the people who lived on after the death of a human bomb, would believe that dead bombers had passed through the point of death and into the world of life after death, thus bringing satisfaction to their influence and fulfillment to their knowledge of life after death. The death of the bombers would confirm the beliefs of the people of influence and strengthen their conviction that they were right about life after death, but then, dead bombers could not tell them otherwise. However, the answer to the question above, on the physiology of thought after death, tells us that the people of influence would only be fooling themselves, human bombs would die as their brains became incapable of thought upon their death.

THE RIGHTS OF HUMAN BOMBS AND PEOPLE OF INFLUENCE

This paradoxical situation makes it difficult to point to ways to eliminate the involvement of human bombs in terrorist tactics. As mentioned previously, one point of attack would be the people who influence humans to willfully become human bombs, but this could not be one point but at least five, clergy, elders, peers, friends, and relatives. All of the people with whom the future human bomb would have contact, more or less all the citizens that compose a culture or civilization. It would be these citizens who would have to convince potential human bombs <u>not</u> to become human bombs, but someone would have to convince this group of citizens that a life after death did not exist and who would that be? The people of influence from the same culture? That would be a first but not very likely choice. The people of influence from another culture? That would more than likely be the case, but cultures with very strong beliefs in a world of life after death and other cultures with different beliefs in a different world of life after death would lead to conflict. Entire populations of nations would be involved and divided, those who believed that humans should have the right to become human bombs, and believed that humans have the right to influence humans to become human bombs on the one hand. On the other hand, we would have those who believed that no one should become a human bomb and no one should influence humans to become human bombs.

Thus, we come to an impasse. Does a human have a right to become a human bomb? Does a human have a right to influence someone to become a human bomb? Does a human have a right to influence those who influence humans to become human bombs? Does a human have a right to influence humans not to become human bombs? The voice of human rights tells us that the answer to all questions is yes.

We can readily see that the elimination of humans as bombs as tactics for intimidation and terror is a problem that will not be solved in the immediate future. Elimination of the source of the tactics, human bombs, is not feasible because the humans supporting and detonating the bombs are thoroughly convinced that they will enter a bountiful life after death after they carry out their missions. The people of influence are so thoroughly convinced that a world of life after death does exist that it will take hundreds to thousands of generations to convince a population that there is no such place as a world of life after death, so the elimination of terror through the people of influence would be the way to go but this would take a vast amount of time, perhaps as long as humans have thought that there might be life after death.

HOW TO ELIMINATE HUMAN BOMBS: IT SEEMED SIMPLE AT FIRST

It seemed simple at first, advertise to the world: Life after death in a world of gods and spirits only exists in the thoughts of humans. It may take a hundred thousand years for humans to realize that their thoughts of gods, spirits, and a life after death are nothing more than thought. A pleasant comforting thought, nevertheless, only thought that will vanish with death. When and if all humans come to a realization that promises of a beautiful life after death, a life without pain, a life without suffering, a life with all that you may desire, cannot exist in a dead human, those thoughts can only exist in the thoughts of a living human brain. If all humans are given this direction by other humans, then terrorists could not use promises of a beautiful life after death to lure humans into killing themselves along with as many other humans as possible. If humans could only come to this realization, they would eliminate terrorists who plot destruction through the deaths of their fellow humans, but we know that it would not be easy to convince people with firmly held beliefs backed by the collective thoughts of millions of people.

It seemed simple at first, advertise in all media over an extended period of time that the world of life after death exists only in the thoughts of living humans with live brains, any form of life after death is an impossibility, even a spiritual life, as explored in Chapter 3. If all the peoples over all of the world could come to this realization, then all of the peoples would come to have a greater appreciation and respect for human life and the life on planet Earth, and there would be no need to solicit humans to serve as bombs. However, we all know that an extensive advertising campaign expounding the impossibility of a world of life after death would meet with unabated opposition from the world wide clergy, and the presidents, citizens, and politicians of most nations. With this approach, the world would remain without an answer to the devastating problem of human bombs.

WHAT ABOUT THE OPPOSITION?

What do we do about the opposition? Convince them to alter their thoughts? That would not be an easy task. If terrorism is to be eliminated, though, the opposition must come to realize that life for humans begins and ends while their brain functions and lives in thought. Those thoughts can conjure gods, spirits, and worlds of life after death, and those thoughts could now be put into words and the words passed from generation to generation and expounded by the people of influence, and soon most humans would come to believe the words or they would be ostracized by the people of influence, and this is what humans have been doing since they invented writing more than five thousand years ago, and gods and spirits in the neighborhood of one hundred thousand years ago. Humans seem to have a great need for their gods, spirits, and worlds of life after death and they have been with us for a long long time. Hence, it will not be easy to convince the opposition to alter their thoughts on the importance of their gods, spirits, and worlds of life after death. However, if human bombs are to be eliminated, the opposition must be convinced that their personal thoughts will not alter the fact that all human thoughts of gods, spirits, and life after death will die when the brain dies.

HUMANS HAVE REVERSED THE ROLES OF GODS AND HUMANS

Even though thoughts of gods and spirits, who live in a world of life after death have been put into words, they had origin in thoughts by living humans. They are comforting thoughts for living humans and should be acknowledged for what they are, comforting thoughts for living humans, but therein lies the problem. Humans have taken their gods and spirits far beyond thoughts in the human brain. They have been extended out of the brain to places that human thought calls "Heaven", "Mount Olympus", "The World of God", "The Spirit World", or "Nirvana". These are some of the sites that extend beyond the world, ethereal places where human thoughts have brought living spaces to their gods and spirits. Human thought has then reversed the positions of humans and their gods and spirits, so that the gods and spirits control the thoughts of humans and make human thought subservient to the thoughts of gods and spirits. Even though the thoughts of gods and spirits are in reality thoughts from a living human brain.

This brings out an interesting thought, do gods and spirits have thoughts beyond human thought? As established in Chapter 3, the gods and spirits of humans cease to exist when thought dies with the death of the human brain, so gods and spirits are entities of human thought, so humans have the ability to give their gods the ability to think but the thoughts of gods and spirits are, in reality, the thoughts of humans. So it is truly interesting, that human thought has reversed the roles of gods and humans. The gods and spirits, and their world of life after death, began as thoughts in the living human brain, but over the centuries thoughts in the brain have given eminence to the thoughts on gods and spirits so that they have been given the role that controls human destiny, and that is what most humans believe. Now thoughts from the human brain give its gods and spirits control over the world and control over the world in which the gods and spirits live and this would be in a world the brain conceives as outside the human body, the world of life after death.

CORRECTIONS ARE IN ORDER

The brain renders thoughts that the gods and spirits live in an extra-worldly extra-human space like Nirvana or the Heavens. This is what needs correction, the human brain with its thoughts on gods, spirits, and life after death must be given the perception that thoughts in the brain have given rise to its gods and spirits, and the world of life after death, these entities do not reside in a world outside the thoughts of the brain but reside within the brain and come under the control of the human brain not the other way around. Humans should come to know that their gods, spirits, and worlds of life after death are thoughts within their own brains, and their acts and abilities should be governed by human thoughts with origin in the human brain. The gods, spirits, and worlds of life after death should not govern human destiny, they are entities of human thought and should be governed by human thought.

The gods, spirits, and worlds of life after death developed in the brains of humans over an exceedingly long period of time. The original thoughts of humans undoubtedly placed the gods and spirits in worlds outside the brain so subsequent generations would automatically accept their placement in worlds outside the brain and this would automatically become the standard. Generation after generation would accept the development of gods and spirits in worlds outside the brain, so it will undoubtedly take thousands of generations to correct these thoughts and for humans to accept the origin of their gods, spirits, and life after death as thoughts from their own brains. At first, this will require people who are able to withstand pressure from clergy, elders, peers, friends, and relatives, and pressure from the collective thoughts of millions of people from all religions that teach the existence of a world of life after death. As pointed out in Chapter 2, god may be the collective thoughts of millions of people with the same thoughts on who and what constitutes god and the world of god. These millions with the same thoughts provide a powerful background of unity that makes it difficult for social humans to accept the thought that gods, spirits, and worlds of life after death originated in the brains of humans and not the other way around. Humans did not originate as objects designed by the gods of humans, or the spirits of humans who live in a world of life after death. If you don't believe as the masses, then you will be ostracized, and this is my reason for saying that it may take thousands of generations for humans to reverse their thoughts on gods, spirits, and life after death and accept these entities as thoughts that originated in the living human brain and not from extraterrestrial gods who had origin in human thought many millennia ago.

THE WORLD OF HUMAN THOUGHT

If all humans came to accept the knowledge that all humans and their ancestors had origin from previously existing humans and their ancestors, then humans might be able to populate the world without recourse to the use of humans as bombs to intimidate and terrorize. It may take a long long time but the world of humans could become the world of human thought, a world without terror, a world without wars, a world without disease and suffering, a world with a bountiful supply of desirable food for all, a world in which love abounds, a world in which sexual desires are fulfilled, and a world in which anger and killing are unknown, but a world in which death is accepted as a part of life without the need for a mythological world of life after death.

HUMANS MADE THEIR GODS IN THE IMAGE OF HUMANS

The world could become the ideal of human thought if the diversity of humans who populate the world could accept the origin of humans as previously existing humans and accept the knowledge that gods, spirits, and worlds of life after death originated as thoughts in the human brain and are therefore human in origin. Humans did not have origin in the image of supernatural gods or by the hands of supernatural gods. The supernatural gods of human thought originated as thought in the human brain, therefore, man made his gods, spirits, and worlds of life after death in the image of humans, and that is the reason the gods of humans are very human in their nature. Humans made their gods in the image of humans, not the other way around.

THE POWER OF HUMAN THOUGHT

If all humans on planet Earth came to the realization that humans made their gods in the image of humans, then humans would have no need to entice other humans to sacrifice themselves for a world that existed only in the minds of humans who had need to intimidate and terrorize their fellow humans because they believed that the gods made man in the image of the gods of man and those gods lived in spiritual worlds that accepted the living spirits of humans after their deaths. Very powerful beliefs that originated in the thoughts of living humans, if those thoughts originated in the brains of living humans, then they had origin in humans, not in supernatural gods, so those beliefs would be false, they did not originate in supernatural gods, but in the thoughts of humans.

CHERISH THE WORLD OF HUMAN THOUGHT

The peoples of the world should be informed, but how many centuries would it take for all humans to realize that humans made their gods in the image of humans with human characteristics. The worlds of life after death are non-existent. The only world for humans is the world in which they live as humans with a brain filled with thought. The elimination of intimidation and terrorism by humans will come to fruition when all humans come to cherish the world of human thought.

Over many thousands and thousands of years human brains of different peoples from different lands and very different backgrounds have thought out many different types of gods and spirits, and different forms of life after death, so it may take as many years for humans to alter their thoughts and come to the realization that past thoughts on gods, spirits, and worlds of life after death are not correct. Humans, on our small planet, Earth, must come to live in peace and harmony without intimidation or terrorist tactics. At some time humans will have to begin to alter their thoughts on their gods, spirits, and worlds of life after death and when will this begin? Tomorrow or in another millennium, or never?

CHAPTER 5

WOMEN SHOULD HAVE CONTROL OF THEIR OVA

EVERY OVUM HAS THE POTENTIAL FOR LIFE

Women abort a potential human life a little more frequently than once a month. Normally, almost every living woman who has entered puberty or passed into adulthood will ovulate approximately every 28 days with the release of a viable living ovum. This ovum has the potential to become a living human. If a human sperm penetrates the membranes surrounding the ovum, then the ovum will be activated, the sperm will bring a second set of chromosomes to the cytoplasm of the ovum and we say that the ovum has been fertilized. When this happens the ovum will go through numerous cell divisions and become an embryo which will develop into a fetus, a new born, a child, an adolescent, and adult. Thus, every ovum has the potential to become a human adult whether it is fertilized or not. However, only those ova that are fertilized will develop into an embryo and on to an adult human if all goes well.

THE FATE OF UNFERTILIZED OVA

What happens to the ova that are not fertilized? They are released into the oviduct and if they do not meet a sperm in approximately the upper third of the oviduct they will not be fertilized. Not meeting a sperm in the oviduct signifies that these ova are doomed. They pass through the rest of the oviduct by ciliary action and muscle contraction, and are released into the uterine cavity. They might disintegrate in the uterus or remain there until menses occurs, at which time they will be discharged from the uterus and pass out of the body without the possibility of developing into a living human. Thus, the fate of all unfertilized ova is death, and they are eliminated from the body by a natural abortion process.

QUESTIONS THAT ONLY WOMEN SHOULD ANSWER

Women's responsibility toward their ova places them in a unique but awkward position, a position that humanity rarely considers. Almost once a month every adult woman ovulates, releases a living ovum that has the potential to give human life, but if that ovum is not fertilized, it is aborted. Is every human female who ovulates responsible for an abortion and death of an ovum, a potential human, if that ovum is not fertilized? If the answer is YES, then many humans would take the stance that every adult woman who ovulates would have the responsibility to see that her ova are fertilized, then they would not be aborted. However, this would be an irresponsible act that would throw the world population into a frenzy, and make women solely responsible for the overpopulation of the world. If the answer is NO, then every woman and even children, many at the age of ten, would be responsible for the death of an ovum, the death of a potential human, every time ovulation occurred and an ovum was released but not fertilized. To take this to an extreme, if a woman ovulated and knowingly prevented fertilization of her ova, would that be considered a homicide? This again places women in an untenable position, and leads to an even more spurious question that relates to the time at which humanity says that life begins. Viable living ova, with the potential for human life, are released at the time of ovulation, however, many humans do not consider unfertilized ova as living viable potential humans until after fertilization, but fertilized ova have no greater potential for human life than unfertilized ova. They both have that potential, even fertilized ova have a long way to go, even the embryonic stages have a long way to go before they can sustain an independent life. These may seem like ridiculous questions, but they are questions that humanity unknowingly forces on women and should be given more than a modicum of thought.

The use of the emotionally charged term, abortion, brings further questions. When should the removal of ova from the female reproductive tract be considered an abortion? Some would say after fertilization but until unfertilized ova pass into the lower part of the oviduct they have the same potential to give human life as fertilized ova. Nevertheless, unfertilized ova will die and will be discharged from the reproductive tract at a later time. Most would not consider this an abortion, rather a natural step in the reproductive process, but viable ova are released to the oviduct and these ova eventually pass into the uterus where they either disintegrate or are discharged from the reproductive tract at the time menstruation occurs. This could easily be considered a natural abortion, but would the removal of FERTILIZED ova from the reproductive tract be an abortion? This could very well be considered an abortion, particularly by men, because fertilized ova also contain part of a male reproductive cell, the sperm head, and that could be the reason humans place greater value on fertilized ova and consider them more sacred. This still leaves us with open questions: When should an abortion be called an abortion? Is surgical removal of unfertilized ova from the oviduct an abortion, or does it become an abortion only after they have been fertilized? These questions truly relate to the responsibilities of women and not to society in general. Questions that only women should answer.

PREGNANCY IS THE RULE FOR NONHUMAN PRIMATES

Humans appear to be the only primates with the problem of aborting unfertilized ova. Nonhuman primates, in their natural habitats, did not develop a menstrual cycle, they have an estrus period during which ovulation occurs. Estrus is also the time at which the female is receptive to copulation and sends signals that attract males. When primates, other than humans, ovulate they are in estrus and actively engage males to deposit their sperm so that their ova will be fertilized at the time they are ovulated. Thus, if female primates are not pregnant and they go into estrus, they will attract males, ovulate, copulate, and under normal circumstances all ova will be fertilized and pregnancy will ensue, so the normal state for primates in the wild would be pregnant.

Every time primates ovulate fertilization of the ova is almost guaranteed so being pregnant or lactating with babies is the normal state. Ova are fertilized, cell division ensues, an embryo develops into a fetus, a baby is born, and the mother lactates. Lactation prevents ovulation of another ovum, the baby feeds on the mother's milk, the baby grows and eventually stops breast feeding, this permits estrus and ovulation, copulation occurs, the new ovum is fertilized, the blastocyst implants in the uterus, and that female primate becomes pregnant again. With primates in their natural habitats, almost all ova would be fertilized and attain their potential to develop into a newborn. The estrus cycle gives them no choice, an ovulated ovum is normally fertilized, so the natural abortion of unfertilized ova would be extremely rare in nonhuman primates.

THE MENSTRUAL CYCLE GAVE WOMEN CONTROL

Somewhere along the evolutionary line to humans, there was a switch from an estrus cycle in primates to a menstrual cycle in human primates. It has not been possible to determine where or when this occurred but it happened, and has placed an additional burden on the human female. A burden that would not be known to the human male. In the menstrual cycle of human females, ovulation occurs normally every twenty-eight days in the middle of the cycle. Copulation may occur at any time in the cycle, so there is no specific time for copulation as there is with an estrus cycle. Thus, women have to make a choice, to copulate at the time of ovulation so that fertilization will ensue, or to prevent the entrance of sperm into the Fallopian tubes at the time of ovulation, and as a consequence prevent fertilization of ova and the development of another human. In other words, women have to make a life or death choice, to permit fertilization and the continuation of the life of their ova, or to prevent fertilization and permit the death of their ova.

The choice to give life or death is a choice that primates other than humans do not have to make, only the human female. Women, who do not become pregnant every time they ovulate, have a natural abortion almost once a month. Just think, if women had an estrus cycle and followed the rule for other primates they would be constantly pregnant or lactating with an offspring and what would that do for the world population? By now it would be so dense that there would be standing room only, so for humans and women in particular, the switch from an estrus cycle to a menstrual cycle permitted control over copulation, hence, control over the life or death of ova and places women in position to control the population. This is certainly an added burden that has been placed on women, but a burden whose control has been usurped by males, religious groups, political parties, and entire governments.

ETHICS AND MORALITY COME TO WOMEN'S OVA

All of these factions have brought morality and ethics to women's ova. If a women's ova are not fertilized, then they naturally abort at least twelve ova a year. That means the death of twelve potential humans. Now, which is morally or ethically correct, to permit the death of a woman's ova through a natural process, and in so doing, kill a potential human but regulate the population of the world; or prevent the death of a woman's ova by permitting fertilization, this would continue the life of her ova and permit the life of another human, and in so doing, over populate the world? By the same token, which would be morally or ethically correct, to permit natural abortion and death of women's ova, hence, the death of a potential human; or permit women to have their ova fertilized, permit development to the blasytocyst stage, and continue the life of the cells of that blastocyst by using them to enhance or prolong the life of another human?

OVA, ETHICS, MORALITY, AND ABORTION

The mere mention of the word abortion immediately raises moral or ethical questions in the minds of many humans. Would there be any difference between the ovulation of an ovum, its passage down the oviduct, its transfer into the uterus where it dies and disintegrates, a natural abortion; and the ovulation of an ovum, its transfer into the oviduct where it is fertilized, it undergoes several cell divisions and develops to the blastula stage while transporting the oviduct, but before it passes into the uterus it is sucked out of the oviduct and transferred to a culture dish where it develops to a blastocyst and some of its cells are used to enhance or prolong the life of another human. Ova, that have developed to the blastula stage, were removed from the reproductive tract before they implanted in the uterus. Would this be an abortion? It might be. In the first instance, the abortion is part of a natural process but results in the death of the ovum, a potential human. In the second case, a preimplantation blastula was artificially removed from the reproductive tract, but the cells of the blastocyst were used to enhance human life. Thus, an ovum, which would have died otherwise, served humanity to its utmost.

Which process was morally or ethically correct? All have their pitfalls, in the case of natural abortion of unfertilized ova, many healthy viable ova that could be used to control diseases, simply go to waste every month. In the case of the removal of fertilized ova from the oviduct, this could be considered an abortion but these ova could continue life and differentiate into living cells that cure diseases. The moral or ethical stance of humans in general really have nothing to do with these cases. The ova actually belong to the women who brought them to maturity in their ovaries and ovulated them at the appropriate time. These are the women who should have control over their ova and they should determine the fate of their ova. It would be up to these women to decide what was within their moral or ethical structure that would permit them to make their decisions as to the fate of their ova.

RETURN THE RIGHT OF CHOICE TO THE WOMEN

Men, religious organizations, political affiliates, and governments make proclamations, declarations, and pass laws that govern the choices that women can make, but would it be possible to circumvent abortion rules and those that govern the use of cells from human blastocysts as stem cells, and return the right of choice to women who nurture and ovulate mature ova. First, a look at the biological situation. Women have many unfertilized ova. These ova have the potential to develop to the blastocyst stage. Would it be unethical or against the rules to remove unfertilized ova or recently fertilized ova from the oviducts long before they were ready for implantation in the uterus? This would only require the consent of the women who owned the ova, and return choice to the women. Then the women could decide what should happen to their ova. No abortion has taken place and no decrees have been violated.

A BETTER TECHNIQUE THAT AVOIDS ISSUES

Before proceeding further with our thoughts, a few technical improvements come to mind. It is not really feasible to attempt to remove fertilized or unfertilized ova from a women's oviducts. It would be extremely difficult to find a single ova in the oviduct or even ova from multiply induced ovulations. Removal of ova from the reproductive tract would not be a very profitable technique.

There is a technique that could circumvent moral, ethical, religious, and political issues, and give back to women their right to decide what they deem appropriate for their ova. The technique of choice would be to prepare the ovaries with hormones. In this way several ova on each ovary will mature. Mature ovarian follicles can be readily recognized as their thinning walls bulge out from the ovary. These can be punctured with a needle and mature unfertilized ova can be collected in the folicular fluid. These ova can be fertilized by bathing them with sperm in a culture dish. After fertilization the ova can be incubated and cultured to the blastocyst stage. This procedure would be totally disconnected from abortion. It involves the procurement of ova from a consenting woman who has control of her ova, in vitro fertilization, and culture to the blastocyst stage. At which point cells of the blastocyst can be used for therapy in humans with need.

WOMEN SHOULD DETERMINE THE DESTINY OF THEIR OVA

A women's ova should belong to no one other than the woman herself, so religious thought, legislation, or the government have no right to claim responsibility for any woman's ova. These organizations often take it upon themselves to become the overlords of women and their ova, but women should be in charge of their lives and their ova. Only women have the ability to produce ova, so when and how they are used should be the prerogative of women. Men don't have the ability to produce ova yet they write laws that govern the fate of women's ova. The United States Government proclaimed that women have no right to determine the fate of their ova. The president and legislators said that there shall be no research or use of human embryos as a source of stem cells, but remember, the source of human embryos is the ova of women. Laws forbidding the use of human embryos for stem cell research were quickly drawn up and passed by the United States Senate and House of Representatives. Here we have the Federal Government, with the signature of the President, passing laws that tell women that their ova cannot be used for the production of stem cells, which could be the most human, the most beneficial form for the cure, yes cure, of many human diseases and/or deficiencies that may have resulted from accidents. Women, other than a few senators and congresswomen, have had absolutely no say in the matter, yet, they are the only source of human blastocysts.

THE MORALITY OF OVA AND STEM CELLS

Legislation and decrees by religious organizations on the fate of women's ova bring out the morality of the issue. The legislation says that it is immoral to use human embryos for stem cell research. On the other hand, women ovulate once a month and give rise to a potential embryo, if the ova is not fertilized it will die and become nothing. Is this a moral waste of good ova? It is certainly morally averse. However, it is the natural course of events that leads to the death of ova, but it is also the natural course of events for the ova to meet sperm and become fertilized. Would it be morally wrong to continue the life of a fertilized ovum by using its cells to differentiate into cells that would benefit another human? I would say that it is morally correct to use fertilized ova if they are made available by the women who produced them. The ova that give rise to embryonic stem cells would continue to live and benefit a fellow human. Otherwise they would die if they weren't fertilized and this could be morally wrong.

THE HUMANITY AND WISDOM OF WOMEN

Men, religious groups, politicians, or governments should not take it upon themselves to control the ova of women. Women should have the responsibility to see that their ova are fertilized and could have the responsibility to see that their ova are used for the development of another human, or used in the cure of diseases. This would be the responsible position. Currently they face the dilemma of permitting their ova to die, a dilemma that no man has to face, or permitting them to be fertilized and live on as an embryo, so, what is wrong with permitting a fertilized ovum to live on as differentiated cells that supply another human with something that makes life possible for that human? That does not require legislation, decrees, or proclamations, only the humanity and wisdom of women.

CHAPTER 6

DIVERSITY

INTRODUCTION

The word diversity has taken on vast importance in recent years but my thoughts on diversity go back some fifty years while I was taking genetics courses in graduate school. At that time the word diversity was not used to explain the benefits of having a population derived from peoples with diverse backgrounds and countries of origin. At that time "diversity" was hidden in genetics, and that was when I formulated ideas on the reason the United States was at the forefront in science, education, literature, entertainment, form of government, freedom of expression, freedom in politics, and freedom in all aspects of everyday life. My idea sprang from the knowledge that the population of the United States consisted of peoples from all over the world and it was the amalgamation of these peoples and the freedom of opportunity made possible by previous generations of diverse peoples that brought out the brilliance of a genetically heterogeneous population. For some time I have had the diverse background of the United States in mind and through my studies have attempted to bring validity to the idea of greatness through diversity and show historically that "diversity" has resulted in advances in civilizations.

ANCIENT GREECE AND ROME

During my studies in art history classes it became apparent that many civilizations throughout the history of civilizations would rise to greatness, then go into decline and never rise again. This provoked my thoughts and led me to explore reasons for the rise and decline of civilizations. The city-states of the ancient greek civilization always seemed to be at war with one another, one would invade the other and then another, but this kept the population genetically diverse and active with original stories, myths, sculptures, gods, vase paintings, and architecture. The Greek Empire didn't begin until Alexander the Great, from Macedonia, took over the greek government in Athens around 342 B.C. At a much later time, the Romans rapidly expanded their territory into an empire similar to but larger than the Greeks, so I bring the two together here.

The expansion of greek and roman territories into empires required the invasion of foreign lands at least while their empires were building. Invading foreign lands would mean contact with people who had a different genetic background. Inevitably, the greeks and romans would interbreed with the peoples in the foreign lands, and move some foreign peoples into the home territories of Greece and Rome. This would introduce new genetic combinations into the greek and roman populations, and greek and roman genes into the foreign populations. This would diversify the genetic backgrounds of both populations, and bring the appearance of persons with mixtures of foreign and greek or roman genes. Acceptance of persons with mixed genetic backgrounds would require the development of an atmosphere in the populous that would accept a mixture of foreign and greek or roman genes. Mixing genetic backgrounds would bring two and more cultures together, so diversification of genetic backgrounds would also bring a mixture of cultural backgrounds.

These thoughts call a little theoretical background to order: Call it Diversity Theory. While a civilization was building, the introduction of new genes into a population would diversify the hereditary background of that population, with diversification both the Greek and Roman Empires flourished, engineering, art, architecture, literature, philosophy, and government saw creations that had never before been seen. Genetic diversification and the creative atmosphere that was eventually generated had to be accompanied by a populace that would support the new creations with enthusiasm, with money, with support from the general population, the rulers and the gods. In other words, genetic diversification had to generate an atmosphere that was conducive to the acceptance of the changes that were taking place. Another form of diversity comes in when one country conquers another country. Invasion of other lands in ancient times would bring culturally diverse peoples together, this would influence the cultural outlook of both the invaders and the conquered, particularly the conquered. Bringing two or more cultures together, brings peoples with different backgrounds and possibly different viewpoints together, something that I call cultural diversity. One more point on conquering countries and genetic diversification, if the genetic background of the conquered country had stagnated through inbreeding over the centuries, then the introduction of new genetic combinations would help vitalize a genetic background that had stagnated.

After a few centuries of mixing, the populace should have a diversified genetic background. Diversification would lead to new thoughts, new ideas, a renewed enthusiasm, and this would lead to ever increasing attention to new ways to do things, new approaches to life, new art, new literature, new architecture, new government, new approaches to the gods. The atmosphere generated by the execution of these new ideas would in itself generate enthusiasm for the perpetuation of the generated atmosphere, atmospheric diversity. New thoughts and ideas would continue to expand and civilization would reach greater heights as long as the genetic background remained diverse, and cultural and atmospheric diversity were generated.

GENETIC DIVERSITY AND THE DECLINE OF CIVILIZATIONS

Genetic diversity theory can also be used to explain the decline of civilizations? Both the Greek and Roman Empires had a similar history and serve as examples. New genes would have been introduced to the greek and roman populations while new territories were being added to their empires. New genetic material would be exchanged and new genetic combinations would arise as long as new territories were added to the empire. However, when the empires reached the limits of practical logistics, new territories were no longer conquered, so new hereditary materials would no longer be exchanged with the conquered populations. At the same time, new combinations of genetic information would continue to arise as the populations that received the new information would continue to interbreed over the next several generations. During this time new ideas and thoughts would continue to contribute to the complexity of the greek and roman civilizations while diversification spread throughout the populace. However, after a period of time the introduction of new heredity combinations would become more and more limited, and with each succeeding generation the populace would slowly but surely become genetically homogeneous with a loss of diversity. This would be particularly true of the elite and peoples who ruled. Their ability to interact with the general population was limited, the people with whom they would exchange genetic information was also limited, so they would suffer the prospect of losing genetic diversity before the general population. The loss of genetic diversity would mean a decline in new ideas and new thoughts, complacency, satisfaction with the status quo, and loss of enthusiasm for change and advancement. Both genetic and cultural diversity would be dead, and along with those atmospheric diversity. Enthusiasm for the continuation of both the greek and roman civilizations would eventually fade. It was during these times that the Greeks were conquered by lesser civilizations, and the Romans destroyed by marauding bands of barbarians from the country surrounding Rome.

ANCIENT EGYPTIANS AND GENETIC DIVERSITY

On a time scale, the ancient egyptians came before the greeks and romans and were a little different. There was no conquered territory, the North and South came together as one empire, they interbred and interbred with the Nubians to the South, their neighbors to the East and with the peoples in the mesopotamian valley, and the egyptians flourished for many centuries with the development of religion, art, agriculture, architecture, math and writing, and governmental organization. For many centuries intermingling of peoples from diverse backgrounds brought genetic histories that enlivened minds and enhanced creativity and brought the development of agricultural innovations that permitted food production to keep pace with the population. Slowly, after many centuries of inbreeding, the genetic diversity that brought new life to the minds of the people was no longer active. The population became genetically uniform and the leadership in dire need of genetic diversity, the egyptian empire declined, but left a vast legacy of its diverse accomplishments in its burials, writings, art, and architectural monuments.

MESOPOTAMIA AND THE MIDDLE EAST

Very similar events occurred in mesopotamia and the empires that flourished and diminished in the Middle East at about the same time the pharaohs ruled egyptian dynasties. The introduction of diversity into their genetic history brought new ideas, new approaches, and enhanced creativity. The empires would flourish for awhile and then decline. As the empires were building, the home territory and newly conquered territories would flourish with the introduction of new genetic combinations, but as the empire expanded further, the genetic background of the people near home base would become more homogeneous because the introduction of new genetic diversity into the home population would diminish over an expansive period of time. Genetic homogeneity in the rulers near the home territory would become ever more prevalent because of inbreeding and the fact that genetic diversity was no longer being introduced to this population. This would result in a decline in interest for innovation and creativity and a decline in all aspects of life and government that once sparked brains to issue forth with new ideas and incorporate the ideas of diverse populations into those of the home territory. When diversity was no longer introduced and genetic homogeneity became the rule, these empires also went into a state of decline never to recover.

A DIFFERENCE IN THE ANCIENT MESOAMERICANS

The ancient civilizations of mesoamerica were more than a little different. The Olmecs, the oldest civilization in Mexico, did not conquer any territory. Instead, small bands of people gathered together to live in "villages", and small groups of people from out in the neighboring jungles kept joining the larger group while it developed into a civilization. Genetic diversity would be enhanced by the addition of small groups of formerly isolated peoples to the larger group even after the development of a civilization. With civilization defined as a society that has developed groups of specialists such as rulers, priests, agriculturists, and groups of particular interest to the archeological record, builders, artisans, and scribes.

The result of diversity in the Olmec civilization made its appearance in the complex carved stone stela that told about their leaders, in the carved figures made from hard green jade and softer stones, they built architectural monuments that still stand today, and left heads with helmets and individualized faces carved on giant stones eight feet in diameter. This must have been in the days when their civilization was in the process of development while the indigenous people were mixing with peoples in the cities and diversity spread over many centuries.

I think the Mayan peoples are probably a continuation of the Olmecs and probably originated in a similar manner with small groups of jungle dwellers gathering into villages. The villages grew larger as more people joined the villages as they specialized into civilizations. The Mayans, though, developed in different and much more extensive areas than the Olemecs and extended over a much greater length of time. The Mayans extended over a period from 1500 BC to their decline in over 800 AD. They clustered in monumental groups in the Yucatan jungles and Belize, all over northern Guatamala, and in the mountains of southern Mexico. They left gifts of many stela, glyphic writing, pyramids with sacrificial alters on top, complex city centers, ball courts, and networks of highways scattered throughout the jungles and mountains.

MESOAMERICA AND THE SPANISH CONQUERERS

The city-states of mesoamerica always maintained extensive trade, slave, and sacrificial exchanges that maintained diversity among their populations. Additional diversity must have been introduced by peoples who came to the Americas from the South Sea Islands and by those who traveled along the Pacific coast from China, Japan, Russia, and the Arctic. With this background of diversity, religion, art, architecture, and government developed to very high levels with ever increasing complexities and population. At its height, the metropolis of Teotihuacan was larger than the city of Paris in France. However, they could no longer produce sufficient food to feed their people, so they went into very rapid decline long before the arrival of the Spanish. Then, the Aztecs started to flourish about two hundred years before the Spanish conquistadors invaded Mesoamerica but with the Spanish came European diseases that greatly reduced the Aztec population. This made it impossible to determine the effects of the introduction of Spanish inheritance into the Aztec population. Unfortunately, the Spanish speaking priests translated the Aztec language as if it was the language of all Mesoamerica for all times. For generations and generations the Aztecs came to be known as the dominate peoples of mesoamerica, when, in reality, populations of non-Aztec peoples from past times, from different areas, with different languages and slightly different cultures dominated Mesoamerica for hundreds of millennia. I mentioned the long reigns of the Olmecs, and in particular the Mayans, and then there are the Zapotecs, Mixtecs, and Toltecs.

The Spanish conquerors came with edicts from Queen Isabela to bring the Catholic religion to the infidels and return with gold treasures conjured in the minds of Europeans, so the people of Mesoamerica were conquered and were treated as a conquered populous. This in itself would suppress the former benefits of a genetically diverse population which was also decimated by European diseases to which they had no immunity. The surviving population maintained a vast distance to the teachings of the Catholic church for twenty years and finally succumbed when the church introduced the "Lady of Guadalupe". The conquering attitude of the Spanish speaking invaders and the Catholic church took over the minds of the Mesoamerican peoples, so the results of the introduction of Spanish diversity to these small populations would never be realized. Remember too, after the Spanish, the French invaded Mexico and then the United States took over; in historical times the peoples of Mesoamerica have never had a chance to experience the developments that their diversity has to offer.

Recall, long before the arrival of the Spanish the people of Mesoamerica domesticated corn, beans, squash, tomatoes, avocados, peppers, chocolate, vanilla, cotton, turkeys, a hairless dog, and more. They domesticated the greatest number of domesticates of any civilization ever to exist. Think, the Italians had no tomato sauces before Cortez returned to Spain with tomatoes from Mesoamerica. They developed a written language, religions with complex gods, and monumental pyramids that rivaled those of the ancient egyptians. The Mesoamericans were diverse groups of people who traded extensively and mixed cultures, and it would have been truly interesting to see how they would have developed if the Spanish conquerors and the Catholic church had not intervened in their development.

EUROPEAN RENAISSANCE

The decline of the Romans, not long after the death of Christ, marked the beginning of the Dark Ages and a period in which genetic diversity would be absent for over a thousand years. The decline of the Romans was accompanied by several hundred years of inbreeding in the population all over Europe and especially in the Roman royalty. During this time creative activity was at a minimum, the clergy was dominant and ruled that everything that needed to be created had been created, the only thing remaining was to make copies and spread the word. It wasn't until around eleven hundred that people began to move from the countryside and small inbred kingdoms with castles into cities and city-states where the people began to mix genes and produce new genetic combinations, which led to genetically diverse populations. Painters, sculptors, poets, writers, translators, architects, priests, popes, and university professors would originate out of this newly established genetic diversity that would lead into the European renaissance. However, it wouldn't be until the later thirteen hundreds that new artists began to appear and new clergy wanted new paintings on the walls of churches, and ordered new altarpieces for the churches. This new group of genetically diverse peoples would supply Europe with artists, writers, clergy, architects, professors and popes for the next six hundred years. Interestingly, it was now the clergy who was promoting new artists and new paintings for the church. This must have meant that the church had developed a new outlook, copies were out, look at the testaments in a new light, the church was establishing a new atmosphere. The peoples of the European Renaissance would be making discoveries for the next two centuries and beyond.

While the Romans and Europeans were in a state of stagnation in the Dark and Middle Ages, it was during the latter part of this period that the seafaring Vikings were actively engaging the coastal populations of the North Atlantic and the large rivers of eastern Europe. Their gods, boats and navigation skills flourished and their raids along the European waterways helped maintain a genetically diverse Celtic culture. After several hundred years of coastal raids, even the Celtics became inbred and lost their desire to conquer, so genetic diversity declined and so did the Celtic culture.

THE MOST DIVERSE? THE UNITED STATES

During the next hundred years, the population of the United States continued to reap the benefits of diversity with the influx of peoples from western Europe. This included large populations from Ireland, including my grandmother, my father's mother, Germany, Poland, Italy, Norway, and Sweden, my mother's country of birth, and people of Jewish background from all over Europe. A large group of people from China also came to the United States during this time but they were not permitted to associate with U.S. citizens nor did they have desires to mingle with peoples in the United States, this would not come until later. These large groups of peoples mingled with the populous of the United States and set the genetic and atmospheric diversity that would result in the appearance of railroads across the country, and the internal combustion engine with automobiles, motor-cycles and roads; these innovations would require the simultaneous development of coal, oil and gas. The telegraph, radio, and telephone would appear, along with photography, movies, the means to distribute electricity and the light bulb. A hundred years of genetic and atmospheric diversity resulted in twenty-five years of invention and innovation that would result in the appearance of basic utilities and goods that would put millions and millions of people to work and that would be used by practically every person in the United States on a daily basis. This was like an economic utopia, these basic industries required people to build them, once built they required millions of people to keep them operational on a twenty-four hour basis, in addition to many millions of other people, the people who build and maintain the operations also use and pay for the basic utilities and goods.

ATMOSPHERIC DIVERSITY

I should expand on atmospheric diversity, it is essential for public support and public understanding. Atmospheric diversity is based on genetic diversity. The development and construction of large scale inventions/innovations requires understanding, support, and utilization by the general population. This requires a population that understands the needs for such inventions, who will support mentally and monetarily the construction of innovations, and who know that such inventions must be used by a very large percentage of the population. Atmosphere in this case means a favorable mood, a favorable mental attitude, a willingness to understand monetary requirements, an understanding that the population has need for the inventions under consideration. This describes the atmosphere, diversity must come from the population. People from many different backgrounds, people with diverse mental attitudes and aptitudes, people with diverse monetary needs, all must bring their thoughts to the same favorable mood of support, this brings diversity to the atmosphere and creates atmospheric diversity, or a favorable mood of support from a diversity of backgrounds. Atmospheric diversity would be dependent on the genetic diversity of the population giving a favorable mood of support. Genetic diversity would give rise to atmospheric diversity, the atmospheric diversity over the entire diverse population that has arisen in the United States would come together with thoughts that would give favorable support to an invention that arose during the time that that genetically diverse population was in existence.

The next groups that brought additional diversity to the population of the United States and set the stage for the next series of large scale inventions/innovations were people from Korea, Vietnam, Taiwan, China, Japan and India. Mixing with the diverse population already present in the United States, peoples from these countries would help create the diverse atmosphere that would sustain the following enterprises for many many years: Rockets, humans in space, humans land on the moon, satellites, computers, software applications, printers, the internet, wireless telephones, wireless internet, globalization of commerce, satellite contact with planets, remote explorers travel the surface of mars.

CONCLUSIONS

Peoples from diverse backgrounds may be brought together by conquest, by peaceful communion of small groups into civilizations, or by migration/immigration into or about developing civilizations or previously existing civilizations. By which means makes no difference in the end the result will be the same. The people will intermingle and breed, and bring diversity to the population, genetic diversity, atmospheric diversity, and cultural diversity. When diversity enters a population, and the three diversities mix together at the same time, very favorable things happen, new ideas arise, new thoughts enter the picture, and innovation sets in. It is a point for enthusiasm to blossom, for new ways to do things, for new approaches to life, new art, new literature, new architecture, and new ways to organize government.

Chapter 7

HIGHLY PIGMENTED SKIN IS AN ENVIRONMENTAL ADAPTATION TO SHADE AND SHADOWS

MELANOCYTES, MELANIN AND SUN LIGHT

The exposure of unprotected human skin to ultraviolet light emanating from the sun can induce a reaction in the skin. The primary reaction is the breakdown of melanocytes (pigment cells) with the release of melanin (the pigment) into the basal layer of the epidermis, the very outer layers of the skin. If exposure to ultraviolet is not extensive, limited to no more than thirty minutes, melanocytes break down, pigment is released, and the production of more melanocytes is stimulated. This would be considered a normal reaction of the skin to exposure to ultraviolet radiation and is part of what is known as "tanning". The same reaction takes place the next time the skin is exposed to strong sunlight, and another layer of melanin is added to the epidermal layer of the skin. This makes the skin darker, and according to myth the melanin absorbs some of the harmful ultraviolet rays and gives protection to the skin. However, the next time the skin is exposed to strong sunlight, the ultraviolet rays in that light again break down more melanocytes and the skin becomes even darker. The same thing happens the next time the skin is exposed, more melanocytes break down and the skin gets even darker. Now it may take a longer exposure but melanocytes still break down. The continued breakdown of melanocytes and the ever darkening of the skin has led me to question the thought that melanocytes in the skin and the release of melanin into the epidermal layers provides protection from ultraviolet rays, which is the statement commonly seen in print and expressed orally.

But, is the primary purpose of melanocytes in the basal layer of the epidermis and the presence of melanin in the outer layers of the epidermis, the squamous epithelium, an adaptation for protection from harmful ultraviolet radiation from the sun, or is the presence of melanocytes and melanin an adaptation for something entirely different?

THE PRIMARY FUNCTION OF MELANIN IS NOT PROTECTIVE

Consider people with high concentrations of melanocytes and melanin in their skin. Do these people suffer from sunburn when exposed to an overdose of bright sunlight? I have known friends and acquaintances with highly pigmented skin and their skin could definitely burn from over exposure to the sun. Observations at poolside and the beach reveal that persons with highly pigmented skin are subject to tanning, or the breakdown of their melanocytes after exposure to bright sunlight. In these instances, the parts of bodies not exposed to sunlight on a near daily basis are noticeably lighter in color than the parts exposed to sunlight on a near daily basis. Furthermore, other friends and acquaintences with skin ranging from slightly dark to dark get darker and darker as the Spring and Summer progress. With these people, the presence of greater concentrations of melanocytes and melanin does not protect melanocytes from breaking down after exposure to bright sunlight. In my mind the protective effect attributed to melanocytes and melanin in the skin of humans is very minor. Common sense tells us that protection must be one of their functions, but this may be an incidental function.

What, then, is the primary function of the presence of higher concentrations of melanocytes in the skin of some peoples of the world?

IN AFRICA DARK SKIN AND HAIR ARE ADAPTATIONS FOR BLENDING WITH SHADOWS

Environments hold the key to this question and in particular the environments in Africa and the areas of the northern hemisphere with deciduous trees. Let us take our thoughts to Africa and a time before humans wore clothes. Look to the lightly forested areas, savannahs, and jungles of sub-sahara Africa. The lightly forested areas have trees and shrubs with dark shadows that contrast with the areas of bright sunlight just outside the shaded areas. The shadows of the sparse population of trees and shrubs on the savannahs would markedly contrast with brightly lighted dry grassy areas. Persons with dark skin and black hair would blend in well with the dark shadows, and the high contrast provided by the bright sun would render these persons practically invisible from even relatively short distances. The jungles would be similar but the contrast between light and shade would not be as great, there would be shadows and very dark shade. Nevertheless, persons with dark skin and dark hair would be very hard to detect in an area that was very darkly shaded. Gorillas and chimps with their black hair and skin are very hard to detect in the dark forests of Africa. A person in the shade could also look out and view all that was taking place in the lighter areas and possibly wait in the darkness in ambush for the next meal. According to these accounts, highly pigmented skin and dark hair would be adaptations for blending with shadows. Areas with high contrast between light and shade would be particularly adept for blending with dark skin and hair. In humans, the adaptation of dark skin and hair could very well be camouflage for shade.

IN THE NORTHERN HEMISPHERE SKIN PIGMENT CHANGES WITH THE SEASONS

What about peoples in the northern hemisphere? Again, think back to a time when humans did not wear much in the way of clothing at least during the late Spring, Summer, and early Fall months. In the Spring, the leaves on the deciduous trees make their first appearance and cast only light spotted shadows. This would be ideal for skin with very little pigment, the bright spots coming through the leaves and branches would appear bright on light skin, and the light shadows cast by the leaves and branches would show up as shadows on light skin. This would provide even better protection from animals with only black and white vision. As the leaves grew the shadows would darken. At the same time, humans with lighter skin would be exposed to sunlight that was getting brighter by the day, exposure to a brightening sun would break down some of the melanocytes in the lighter skin so it would turn darker and complement the darkening shadows of the trees. As Summer approached, the tanning reaction in light skinned humans would turn their skin darker with each day that it was exposed to brighter sunlight until it was very dark. With Summer the darker skin would blend with the darker shadows of fully leaved trees, and the bright sun would bring out the contrast between light and shade and provide these humans with shadow camouflage as it did with the highly pigmented skin of humans in Africa all year around. In the Fall, ultraviolet rays that reach the surface of the Earth from the sun would begin to diminish, the quantity of pigment in light skinned humans would also diminish and their skin would become lighter. This would also coincide with leaves falling from deciduous trees in the Fall, the shadows and contrast would not be so great as in the Summer, but the lighter skin would blend with the light and shade of trees with fewer leaves. In the northern hemisphere in the Winter months, the humans living at this time would probably wear clothing so the quantity of pigment in their skin would be less than at any other time of the year, but wearing clothing would make this irrelevant. However, light skin in Winter could be disadvantageous, their light skin would stand out if they were in the shadows of tree trunks, or in forests, or standing in front of dark tree trunks or shrubs. Clothing the color of tree trunks could be an advantage in the Winter.

CHANGES IN SKIN PIGMENT FOLLOW THE SUN CYCLE

In the northern hemisphere, the skin of lightly pigmented humans becomes darker as Spring blossoms from Winter and the sun becomes increasingly brighter. By Summer the skin of light skinned humans has become very dark and blends with the dark shadows of trees, but with the passing of Summer and the approach of Fall, the power of the Sun diminishes and the skin becomes light again. Thus, changes in the skin follow the yearly cycle of the sun as its ultraviolet power increases from Spring to Summer, and decreases from Summer to Fall. At the same time, changes in the quantity of pigment in the skin follow the yearly cycle of deciduous trees as they establish increasingly dark shadows as they progress from leafless to small leaves and light shadows in the Spring, and then to the fully leaved condition and dark shadows in Summer, and on to the Fall with falling leaves and light shadows.

SKIN PIGMENT SERVES AS CAMOULFLAGE IN SHADE

The quantity of pigment in the skin definitely appears to be an adaptation to shade. In the bright sun of Africa, humans developed highly pigmented skin and dark hair that blended with deep shadows that contrast with the bright sun. The use of a consistent and readily available environment with which to blend, namely shade or shadows, would offer convenient places to escape detection, or places that could serve as a hidden site for the ambush of prey. This would give humans a distinct advantage. In the northern hemisphere, changes in the darkness of the skin correlate well with the brightness of the sun, with changes in the darkness of the shadows of the trees and shrubs, which in turn is dependent on changes in the foliage of leaves on the trees which is dependent on the changing seasons. It is unavoidable, pigment in the skins of humans is an adaptation to shadows or degrees of shade. In the northern hemisphere, this developed along with the development of light skin that could change to dark skin as the shade of trees and shrubs became darker or lighter with the changing seasons and serves to show that pigment in the skin is an adaptation to shade. The protective action of Melanocytes and melanin against ultraviolet rays would be incidental to their role as camouflage in shadows and shade.

CHAPTER 8

PHEROMONIC THEORY:INDIVIDUALITY, SEXUALITY, AND LOVE

INTRODUCTION

Pheromones, what are they? Odorless airborne compounds that contain carbon, relatively complex compounds that are very volatile but stable for short periods of time. These compounds are secreted by the body into the air where they pass to other individuals who may be stimulated, attracted, or inhibited by these airborne compounds, some refer to them as airborne hormones. To be active, pheromones must be part of a two part pheromonic system: The volatile pheromonic chemicals themselves, and just as important, the specific receptors to which they bond. Pheromones would be useless without receptors to stimulate the recipient. In summary Pheromones are secreted into the air by one individual, bond to receptors found on another individual and in so bonding, inform the recipient that an individual of the same species, from the same regional territory, from the same or the opposite sex is present in the distant or immediate vicinity. They are often called sex attractants, but I believe that they give information beyond sex.

The pheromonic receptors give the bearer the ability to follow a concentration gradient. The gradient is established by the individual secreting the pheromone., it will be in highest concentration at the source and diluted by the air as the distance from the source increases. For instance, at 1000 yards from the source we set the pheromone concentration at 10 parts per billion molecules of air, at 900 yards the concentration would increase to 100 parts per billion, and at the source the concentration would be 1000 parts per million. The bearer of the receptors might bind one molecule of pheromone at 1000 yards, two molecules of pheromone at 900 yards, 10 molecules at 500 yards, and overwhelm the receptor system with a 100 molecules of pheromone at the source. The increase in the number of pheromones bound with the decrease in distance from the source (the gradient) would inform the bearer that the source was getting closer. If the recipient with the receptors, directs movement toward the increase in the number of molecules bound, then the source will become ever closer. Thus, the pheromonic receptors give direction toward the bearer and tell if the bearer is far or near, while the pheromones themselves stimulate the receptors and prepare the host for action through stimulation of the nervous system.

Now that we have a basic understanding of the definitions of pheromones and how they work, we should ask: What is their value to the human population?

SPECIES IDENTITY

Pheromones can establish species identity. The pheromones produced by one species will bond only to the receptors of the same species, which means, the pheromones and receptors will be species specific. The pheromones of one species will not bond to the receptors of another species, therefore, they will not attract members of other species but will inform members of the same species about the presence of members of the same species, so they aid in establishing species identity. Here, only one type of receptor and one type of pheromone would be required by the species. A species pheromonic system would be important for species to herd and gather together, or to repel or avoid gathering together.

ANCESTRAL AND TERRITORIAL IDENTITY

Down the scale one unit, we have another pheromonic system that identifies large groups of persons such as races, or groups of people who have been isolated from other groups for long periods of time, or groups of people who have reproduced together for a very long period of time, say several millennia. These groups will produce a specific pheromone that will be detected by specific receptors of the same groups and will inform the members of the same groups that they are in the presence of people who share the same group pheromones. In other words, people who share the same pheromones and possess the same pheromonic receptors. This would be the reason that peoples who have shared the same geographical territory for centuries, and have bred together, have a natural tendency to gather together, to socialize together, to marry together at the exclusion of peoples who have not shared that territory for centuries. Nevertheless, we must keep in mind that pheromones are genetically determined, and peoples from all over the world have their origin in common ancestors, so a number of persons from all isolated territories will have group pheromones and group receptors that extend beyond their own territory and match those from distant territories. This permits diversity and predicts that diversity will increase as group pheromones and group receptors become more diverse as people from distinct territories come together to reproduce.

PHEROMONES AND HETEROSEXUAL IDENTITY

A third type of pheromonic system is for sexual identity. This requires a four part system: Pheromones to identify females, these would be secreted by females; pheromones to identify males, these would be secreted by males; pheromonic receptors for bonding female pheromones, these would be the predominant types found with males; pheromonic receptors for bonding male pheromones, these would be the predominant types found with females. In humans, the most straight foreword combination for heterosexual males would be males with pheromonic receptors for female pheromones. The pheromones would bond to the female receptors and stimulate the nervous and reproductive centers of the male and inform males that females were nearby. For females, they would have receptors for male pheromones, when male pheromones bonded to the male receptors in the female, they would have a stimulatory effect on the female's nervous and reproductive centers, and inform her that males were in the vicinity.

This would be a very straight foreword system without many possibilities for error. I don't believe that it is quite so simple. A more likely scheme would be the presence of both receptors in the same individual. For male heterosexuality, ninety percent of the receptors would be for female pheromones and ten percent for male pheromones. This would attract males to females. If bonded to male pheromones, the small percentage of male receptors might have an inhibitory effect on the nervous and reproductive centers and serve to repel other males. For female heterosexuality, ninety percent of the receptors would bond male pheromones and stimulate the nervous and reproductive centers of the females, and inform females that males were nearby. This would attract females to males. Like the males, the presence of a small percentage of female receptors in the female might have a repelling effect toward other females and enhance heterosexuality. Thus, in approximately ninety percent of human males and females, pheromones identify sex and aid in bringing males together with females, in other words help to establish heterosexual reproductive activities.

PHEROMONES AND HOMOSEXUAL IDENTITY

Hereditarily defined pheromones and their receptors can describe homosexuality and bisexuality. For homosexuality, the number of receptors becomes reversed. For males, ninety percent of the receptors would bond male pheromones and ten percent would bond female pheromones. This would stimulate the nervous and reproductive systems of males and attract males to males. In this instance, ten percent of the receptors that bond female pheromones could act as a repellent and inhibit male to female attraction. Likewise for female homosexuality, ninety percent of their receptors bond female pheromones, so they would be stimulated by and attracted to females. Again, the small percentage of male receptors in these females, when bonded to male pheromones, could have an inhibitory effect toward males and further enhance homosexual attraction.

One other possibility comes to mind, again hereditarily determined. The pheromones themselves are reversed but the receptors remain heterosexual. In this instance males would synthesize and secrete a preponderance of female pheromones rather than male pheromones. The female pheromones would bond to the female receptors present in normal males. This would set up an attraction between males who secrete female pheromones and normal males who normally have female receptors that bond female pheromones. This would establish a homosexual attraction between males. Likewise for females, they would synthesize and secrete an abundance of male pheromones rather than female pheromones. The male pheromones would bond to the male receptors normally present in heterosexual females. This would establish an attraction between females who secrete male pheromones and females who normally have male receptors, or a homosexual attraction between females. This could be very confusing because these males and females have normal receptors, the males have female receptors and the females have male receptors. The males secrete female pheromones so these could, and probably do, bond to and mask their own female receptors. These individuals may never have an opportunity to bond with male pheromones secreted by normal females.

PHEROMONES AND BISEXUAL IDENTITY

A pheromonic system can also define bisexuality. This is an easy case on paper, here, fifty percent of the receptors in both males and females bond male pheromones and fifty percent of the receptors in both males and females bond female pheromones. The pheromones of both males and females would stimulate the nervous and reproductive systems of both males and females, this would establish an attraction to both males and females, hence, a bisexual state. I should point to an obvious condition, a continuum from fifty percent to ninety percent, bisexual to homosexual, and another continuum from bisexual to heterosexual. Thus, pheromonic systems can define the spectrum of sexuality from homosexuality to bisexuality to heterosexuality, all under genetic control.

PHEROMONES AND LOVE

Did you ever wonder why people don't develop a loving relationship with everyone that they get to know? Is there a reason for this? During a lifetime we develop relationships that involve love with only a very few people that we get to know well, and pheromones can play more then a significant role. A pheromonic system exercises a very definite role when it comes to love. This is because pheromones can give identity down to the individual. Each individual passes pheromones into the air, these pheromones or a combination of pheromones have a chemical structure that identifies the individual. Each individual has a pheromonic receptor or receptors that will only bond to the pheromones that match that receptor and they will be the pheromones that define another individual. When these pheromones bond to their receptor they send a signal to the pleasure and love centers of the brain that tell the individual with the stimulated receptors, this is a person who brings pleasure and love, and automatically stimulates my brain and senses. What one hopes for, in this instance, is a match between the pheromones of the individual with the stimulated receptors, and the receptors of the individual who exuded the pheromones that made the match with the other individuals receptors. In other words, the ideal is to have two people with matching pheromones and matching receptors. I refer to this as pheromonic love. It is rather rare but it happens frequently and when it happens love is inevitable, strong, and most of the time everlasting, sex is constantly stimulated and immediately strengthens the love bond. I believe that one instance of such a match was between my youngest sister and her husband. They met as teenagers in high school, married, had loving children, and grand children, and remain sexually and lovingly married to this day.

Matching pheromones with matching receptors would be the strongest case of pheromonic love, but with most biological systems this would be an over simplification, there are probably many levels of pheromonic love. I usually refer to pheromones and their receptors in the plural and I believe this to be the case. With pheromones that define the individual and love let us say that there are six pheromones and six receptors. The strongest match would be six pheromones matching and bonding to six receptors in one male and one female. A strong but weaker match would be six pheromones bonding to four receptors in one person and six pheromones bonding to five receptors in the other person. This would also lead to a very strong love relationship. The length of an encounter would also be important. In a brief encounter, one or two matches might take, but in a lengthy encounter the two receptor systems might become saturated with five out of six matches. A mixed reaction would also be possible. In mixed company, three different males might each exude two pheromones that bond to a six pheromone receptor system inherent in one female. The pleasure and love centers of this female would be stimulated and she would probably feel that she was having an enjoyable time in the company of these three males, but she wouldn't be able to determine if she was responding to any one of the males. If this same female exuded three different pheromones that bonded to one of the receptors in each of the three males, the males would be attracted to this female but very weakly. This would be a rather mixed reaction with no clear responses. A very weak match would be the transpiration of six pheromones with only two bonding to two receptors in one individual and the secretion of six pheromones with only one bonding to one receptor in the corresponding individual. This would not result in a love relationship. All combinations would be possible not just those used as examples in this discussion. The weaker matches would undoubtedly be the case with most of the people that a person would encounter in the course of a day, and this is the reason we don't develop a love relationship with every individual that we get to know or pass on the street.

PHEROMONES AND INCEST

Another activity that could be attributed to pheromones is the prevention of incestuous relationships. Here, I identify groups of individuals with pheromonic identity, namely, families. Families develop a pheromonic system that identifies the family. Members of a family would have a similar genetic background and should have the ability to synthesize family pheromones and make receptors that would be derivatives of the family pheromones of both the mother and father. Family pheromones would bond to family receptors and this would lead to an inhibition of the sex drive and reproductive centers in the brain.

In my observations of human families there appears to be a very natural tendency for family members to avoid sexual contact. This appears to be natural and not something imposed by outside sources such as laws, societies, or religions. This natural tendency could be explained by applying pheromonic theory. Members of an immediate family, mothers, fathers, brothers, and sisters are genetically linked so they could have another set of pheromonic receptors and pheromones that would identify family. These pheromones and receptors would have an inhibitory action on reproductive centers and the sex drive. The close living conditions of a family would normally keep the family receptors fairly well saturated with family pheromones, and thus, inhibit the sex drives that family members could have toward one another.

In greater detail, members of a family would be subject to exposure to the family pheromones on a daily basis, this would permit daily bonding between the family pheromones and their receptors, and daily inhibition of the sex drive between family members. The strongest reaction should be between brothers and sisters because they should have pheromones and receptors from both the mother and father. The reaction of brother and sister pheromones to the mother and father might be half that between brother and sister because the mother and father would only have receptors for pheromones of the maternal or paternal type, not for both. Naturally, the mother and father should not have inhibitory family pheromones and receptors because their families extend back to different families and different mothers and fathers. Thus, inhibitory family pheromones and receptors should not be inhibitory to the mothers and fathers. They will still have the pheromones and receptors that serve as love attractants, stimulate the sex drive and keep love alive.

The inhibition of the sex and reproductive centers by interaction between family pheromones and their receptors would extend out to other family relatives. Grandmothers and grandfathers should have the same family pheromones as the mother and father, so brothers and sisters should react to grandmothers and grandfathers as strongly as to mothers and fathers. Aunts and uncles related by heredity should have the same pheromonic systems as the mother and father and should react to the pheromones of brothers and sisters the same as the mother and father. The family pheromonic systems of cousins should be diluted by a generation, so pheromonic interaction and inhibition of sex and reproductive centers should be half of the reaction to their mothers and fathers and aunts and uncles. Pheromones could explain the natural inhibition of incest within family groups.

Exceptions to the natural rule of pheromonic inhibition of family incest do occur. How do we explain instances where incest enters the family relationship? The obvious explanation would be an alteration of the family pheromonic system. Either the family pheromones from the children were altered chemically (genetically), so they no longer bonded to the family receptors of the parents, or the receptors in the children were modified so that the pheromones of the parents no longer bonded to the receptors of the children. Either way, it would lead to a breakdown of the natural inhibitory reaction that occurs when family pheromones bond to family receptors that might lead to incest. This would be equivalent to a situation in which a child failed to produce family pheromones. If it was a female child, she would not synthesize the family pheromones that bonded to the father's family receptors, so there would be no natural inhibitory reaction of a father to a daughter and incest could occur. However, the daughters should still have receptors to family pheromones from the father, so the fathers pheromones could bond to the daughters receptors and elicit an inhibitory response in the daughter. This might be the reason we see the entrance of guilt feelings in daughters if incest did occur. By the same token, if a female child did not synthesize family pheromones, she would not have pheromones that would bond to the natural inhibitory receptors of brothers either, so this would open the possibility of incest between brothers and sisters. However, as with the fathers, the sisters should still have male family receptors for pheromones from their brothers and should still have an inhibitory response, but in this instance, there would be no natural pheromonic inhibition on the part of the brothers. These are a few of the possible combinations that could lead to incestuous relations with the involvement of abnormalities in pheromones and pheromonic receptors.

TRUST YOUR PHEROMONES

The response of centers in the brain to the interaction of pheromones and their receptors may be relatively weak when compared to the power of thought. Pheromones might introduce two brains to love and sustain a pheromonic stimulation of the brain to love for many years, but if the brain perceives ill advised actions it has the power to overcome the pheromonic stimulation of love and bring that love to a close. Similarly, in cases of incest, if bonding between family receptors and family pheromones inhibits sexual advances among family members, then in instances, sexual thoughts or thoughts of power by the brain overpower pheromonic inhibition and incest results. The brain probably has the power to conceive of love on its own by centralizing information on what it perceives as beauty, what it likes in the way of sight and sound, what it conceives as pleasant to the touch, what it considers stimulating to thought, and it probably keeps track of how these things stimulate its pleasure centers. Keeping all of this information in proper perspective would be a task of great demand even for the brain, so the brain may rely on an ancient chemical reaction between pheromones and their receptors to call attention to a possible choice for love. Such things could be conceived as a battle between the mighty power of the brain and weak pheromonic forces trying to influence that great power. This brings out one great difficulty with pheromonic systems in humans, the human brain is sufficiently powerful to override all basic pheromonic responses. When it comes to love, though, I say: "Trust your pheromones."

CHAPTER 9

HOW I STOPPED SMOKING

DUPED BY CIGARETTE COMPANIES AND SOCIETY

I didn't take up the cigarette smoking habit until I was over twenty-one and only began to smoke when I started going out with women who smoked and continued to smoke at least two packs a day for about the next thirty years. According to the movies of the time and cigarette ads, it was the sexy thing to do, it was the social thing to do, and it was the healthy athletic thing to do, so I felt that I was finally joining societal norms, but in reality it was the most stupid thing that I ever did, but I had been duped by the cigarette companies and a society that condoned nicotine addiction.

RECOGNOZING THE SYMPTOMS: TIME TO STOP

After joining the faculty at Harvard Medical School I decided that it was time for me to stop the nasty filthy unhealthy habit of smoking cigarettes. It was also at this time that I noticed that my glottal reflex was becoming confused. At times, not when I was eating but when I took a single swallow of water or saliva, my glottis would not close until after some of the fluid entered my trachea, then I had difficulty getting my glottis to open to expel the fluid, and my cough reflex didn't operate automatically as it should. I had to force my glottis open with pressure from muscular tension on my abdomen while working the muscles in my throat. Once my glottis was open, I had to forcefully keep it open to be able to suck in a little air and slowly suck in more air until my glottis opened fully. Then I could force a cough and remove most of the fluid. A few tiny drops of fluid would remain in my trachea and slowly move into my throat by the action of the cilia that line the trachea. I would think to myself: "Thank goodness, the cilia in my trachea haven't been damaged by the cigarette smoke." I have to stop smoking these stupid cigarettes. Then, I started mentally and physically preparing myself to stop smoking cigarettes.

SWITCHING FROM CIGARETTES TO A FILTERED PIPE

The first thing that I did was to switch from cigarettes to a pipe, no more cigarettes. I looked over the pipes in a tobacco store and selected a very handsome sand blasted briar pipe with a rather large bowl. This was the best looking pipe that I ever bought and it stayed with me all through my pipe smoking years and beyond. I also purchased a pack of pipe tobacco that was recommended by the shop keeper, according to him it was supposed to be a mild aromatic tobacco, I believe it was a pouch of "Mixture 79". When I got outside the store, I filled the bowl of the pipe a little over half full and put a match to it. I pulled the smoke through the stem and it hit my tongue. Yoow! Did it ever burn. It did have a pleasant aromatic odor and flavor, but I later learned that it was the aromaticity that gave it the bite.

The burning sensation on my tongue could be enough to make a person stop smoking but I didn't stop there. I went into a drug store and bought several different small pouches of different kinds of tobacco. While there, I discovered pipes that had disposable replaceable paper filters that fit right into the pipe stem. I bought one of those and tried it with one of the new tobaccos. That was much better, practically no bite but the odor and flavor weren't as pleasant as the aromatic. That day I smoked the pipe with the filter until bedtime and then opened it to see what the filter was doing. The filter was wet and totally dark brown, I was surprised to find that the filter was actually removing that much stuff from the smoke. I cleaned the pipe, replaced the filter and put it away for the night.

THE FILTERS TURNED DARK BROWN

The discovery of pipes with filters, led me to abandon the handsome sand blasted briar, but I kept it as a decoration and would smoke it a few times a year. Eventually, I found that I could cut chemical filter papers to the appropriate length, roll them tightly and insert them into the filter pipes. After insertion, they would unroll a little to make an air passage that was just right. These were cheap, easy to make, and did a good job of filtering the smoke and absorbing condensates. This was what I would use most of the time and could readily replace the filters several times a day when I observed that they were turning very brown or getting wet. I don't really know if these filters ever removed harmful or addictive substances from the smoke but they were removing materials that turned the filters very dark brown. Think, if the filters weren't in place, that brown stuff would pass through the pipe, into my mouth, and into my lungs.

BRAIN WASHED BY ADVERTISING AND MOVIES

Over the years I found some very delightful tobaccos with pleasant tastes and flowery smells. After finding these types of tobaccos, I wondered why I never tried these tobaccos instead of cigarettes and came to the conclusion that I was brain washed by cigarette advertising and the movies and didn't even think about stepping beyond the information that was presented in ads and commercials. I was convinced that cigarettes were the way to go until I decided that I had to eliminate smoking cigarettes from my daily activities. It wasn't until that time that I looked beyond cigarettes and found filtered pipes and delightful bulk tobaccos.

IT WAS TIME TO STOP

I didn't lose sight of the purpose of switching from cigarettes to pipes but I did smoke those pipes with filters for around five years with absolutely no cigarette smoking. By this time even the smell of cigarette smoke brought a note of unpleasantness to my brain. After five years with the pipe, it was time to stop smoking all together. That Fall I met with a fairly nasty virus, the kind that attacks sinuses, nasal passages, throats, and lungs, the kind that makes smoking an unpleasant experience. That was when I cleaned my pipes for the last time, put them in a drawer and never smoked again. To my amazement I didn't have withdrawal symptoms of any kind and lost the desire to smoke, but I truly wanted to stop and did. The absence of after effects could very well be attributed to smoking pipes with filters before I stopped but I will never really know. I know now that it was the best thing that I could have done and felt great relief that I no longer had to stop what I was doing to pull out a cigarette or fill a pipe to satisfy that urge to pull smoke into my mouth, pass it into my lungs, and blow it back out, all for the burden of smoke and nicotine addiction.

THE EASIEST WAY TO STOP? NEVER START

By way of post script, you should never ever start smoking cigarettes or a pipe. The easiest way to stop smoking: NEVER START.

Chapter 10

THE IMPORTANCE OF IODINE

DISCOVERING THE VALUE OF IODINE

When I was a mere child of 8 to 9 years, neighborhood friends and I would play catch with a baseball on the expansive playgrounds of the school next door. We didn't play with the large softball variety but with the so called "hardball" with the red stitching that sewed the leather skin over the ball. It was the kind that was used by the professional baseball players. As a matter of fact, some of them may have come from the professional games that my dad would take us to every now and then on a bright Spring or Summer afternoon when the work was slow. We all had professional type gloves and took meticulous care of them by treatment with "Neats Foot Oil" and keeping them in their special place in the closet with a ball tucked into the pocket. My special glove was the "catchers mitt" even though I never did use it as a catcher in a game. I simply liked to play catch with that kind of glove while most of the other kids liked first baseman's gloves.

During the Summer and Fall, before the world Series would start, we would get out our balls and gloves and throw the ball back and forth and around several times in the course of a week. The Summer of my eighth to ninth year I noticed the beginning of a growth in the palm of my catching hand (left) down about an inch from where my two middle fingers joined my palm. This was almost right in the middle of the spot where the ball would meet my hand when I caught it. It was small at first and didn't hurt when I caught the ball, but as Summer progressed into Fall it enlarged into a hard mass that was growing inward and not out, and it hurt every time the ball hit it. I thought that it was a "wart" but warts usually grow out, not in, so this was a little puzzling. I kept my eyes and ears open for information on warts and looked them up in an encyclopedia. I found that warts could grow inward as well as outward and settled on a wart that grew inward.

While the World Series was in progress I decided that the wart was a real nuisance and had to go, but how could I get rid of it? My mother had some stuff that I knew she used on the corns on her feet so I tried that for awhile, but nothing happened. I knew about tincture of iodine because mother had used it on cuts and wounds, and I knew that it stung when applied to cuts, and my folks always had a bottle in the medicine cabinet. I looked over the small familiar little brown bottle with its menacing skull and cross bones and knew that meant it was poisonous. If it was poisonous and killed germs, I thought that it just might get rid of that wart on the palm of my hand. I took the bottle from the shelf, unscrewed the cap with the applicator attached and applied tincture of iodine to the center of that ingrown wart. It spread over the wart area but didn't go out over the regular skin. I let that dry and gave it another dose, now it was dark brown and to my surprise it didn't sting, and I thought that was good. The next day I gave it another dose until it was dark brown. For about the next two weeks, I gave it a daily dose of iodine and then stopped, in the third week the wart fell out and was gone for good, the cavity filled in with time and left no scar.

A year or so later, another ingrown wart appeared on the same palm. This time I knew exactly what to do and started treatment early and eliminated that wart within two weeks. Since the elimination of the second wart, I have never had another wart on any place on my body.

IODINE AND HERPES SIMPLEX

Using tincture of iodine to get rid of warts was a big discovery for me, but my use of iodine didn't go further than that for quite a few years, when I was an adult in graduate school. Once in a great while I would get a herpes simplex virus right at the entrance to my nasal passages and above my upper lip on the ridges that are remnants of the fusion of three tissues that form the upper lip. On one of these occasions I remembered what tincture of iodine did to warts and decided to try iodine on one of these herpes pustules. I got my little bottle of tincture and applied a good dose to the red area that was beginning to get sore. It burned a bit but didn't sting like it did on cuts, this was to be expected because the skin was not broken at that point. I applied more iodine before going to sleep late that night and noticed that the herpes was no larger than it was when I applied the first dose. It looked like the iodine was preventing the spread of the herpes to surrounding cells. The next morning I could see three little areas where pustules had appeared. This time when I applied the iodine I purposely pressed harder with the tip of the applicator and broke the pustules. Then it did sting and a little pus adhered to the tip of the applicator. I wiped off the tip with tissue and stuck the applicator back in the bottle of tincture to sterilize it. A little serum kept oozing out for about thirty minutes. I blotted this with tissue and noted that the soreness had disappeared. I applied another good dose of iodine after the serum stopped oozing, and this really did sting but I was prepared. Late that night I applied another dose of iodine and noted that all swelling was gone and the herpes sore was gone, now a little scab formed and that was gone in a week.

After this I always treated my herpes with tincture of iodine and refined the technique over the years. Most of the time I would take a pin, sterilize the tip with tincture of iodine, then with the pin tip scratch the area that was turning red and swelling and the area a little way out from the swelling. If the scratching was right a little serum would come out of the scratched area and then I would apply iodine. Most of the time a pustule would never form and the herpes sore would disappear, but if it was not caught at an early time and a pustule formed, I would scratch and break the surface of the area with the pustules, apply iodine to the sore and sterilize the pin by dipping it into the tincture. Serum would ooze from the sore, I would wipe this with tissue and apply more iodine. I would repeat this until serum stopped oozing, the soreness would disappear, and no more pustules would appear. I found that I could prevent a scab from forming if I applied a small dab of petroleum gel to the herpes sore. The gel was an ointment that contained three antibiotics. I don't think the antibiotics did anything, it was the petroleum gel that prevented the healing sore from drying out. In the morning I would apply the gel after applying a dose of iodine. In the evening I would wipe the gel off with clean tissues and noted that serum and tissues that would form a scab were soft and white and would wipe away when I wiped the petroleum gel away. After this, I would apply another dose of iodine and place another dab of petroleum gel on the area where herpes was trying to break out. About three days of this treatment and the herpes would disappear. I am not absolutely certain, but over the years my observations tell me that a herpes sore did not make an appearance in a place where it appeared before and was treated with iodine and petroleum gel. Furthermore, when I first started using iodine to treat herpes it would appear one to two times a year, that diminished to no more than once a year, and more recently to once in three to five years with very small readily treatable sores.

PIGMENTED AREAS AND "LIVER SPOTS"

I have a small (one fourth inch diameter) highly pigmented area on one cheek of my face. If I treat this area with tincture of iodine once a day for two days, and then wait for five days, a patch of skin the size of the pigmented area will slough off or can be peeled off as a thin pigmented piece of cornified epithelium. It will have a slightly brown color and the area on my cheek will be noticeably lighter. If I consistently treat this pigmented area with iodine, it will get lighter and lighter with each passing week but has never totally disappeared, and if I stop treatment, which I do frequently, it turns very dark brown once again but has never increased in size.

Along this same line, I have treated "liver spots", lightly to deeply pigmented areas on the surface of the skin that usually have an irregular shape, with tincture of iodine. I have treated them with one heavy application of tincture on one day and another application on the next day (just as with the small dark brown area on my cheek), stopped this treatment after the second application, and about five days later the outer layers of cornified epithelium (very outer layers of skin) over the liver spot sloughs off taking some of the pigment along. After the epithelium comes off, I repeat the application of iodine for two days and wait for the epithelium to slough just as before, usually about five days. I repeat this process from two to five times. With each application the liver spot gets lighter and lighter in color. Some are gone after two applications while others might take five. Sometimes the liver spots return after several months but I have had others that have never returned.

IODINE, AN ITCHY RASH, AND JELLY FISH

A number of years back, when I was going to the Marine Biological Laboratory in Woods Hole for

Summer research, I contracted an itchy rash all over my back, especially the areas over my shoulders and down to my belt line, but limited to this area. It didn't come over my shoulders to the front, or ever extend around to the sides or front of my torso, or go below my belt line. I think that this particular rash was the result of a swim in Buzzards Bay the day before I was to leave Woods Hole to travel by car to Southern California. I only noticed a slight itch to my back that same night before going to sleep. The next day I started my highway journey back to California and after several hours of travel my back became very itchy and I rubbed it against the back of the seat for partial relief. On my first stop for gas and bladder pressure relief I took off my shirt in the restroom to look in the mirror and noticed pieces of cornified epithelium on the back of my shirt. I looked in the mirror to see a slightly reddened back with bits of epithelium sloughing off. I immediately told myself that this required immediate attention. I found the nearest drug store, bought several small bottles of tincture of iodine, and found a back scratching stick made from bamboo. It was long enough to reach over my shoulder to my back and all the way down to my belt. I located another restroom, went into one of the toilet stalls, tied a piece of cloth around the scratching end of the backscratcher, took off my shirt, poured iodine on the cloth and rubbed an abundance of tincture all over my back. It didn't burn, felt cool and soothing, and stopped the itch. When I stopped for the night, I took a good look at my back and saw big flakes of brown skin hanging from places all over my back. These flakes were drier than I observed earlier and I attributed that to the iodine. Once again I drenched my back with tincture of iodine before going to sleep that night. When I woke up in the morning I saw that the bottom bed sheet was rather tan colored from the iodine, and thought to myself, "nice that I will be sleeping in motels for the next several nights". This gave me a clue that I should wear an older T-shirt under my shirt while my back was being treated with iodine. I dowsed my back with iodine that morning, noted that the iodine brought the itching under control, and that the flakes of epidermal tissue were dry and breaking away from my back by the thousands. I continued the iodine treatment in the morning and at night for the next three days and saw millions of dry flakes of skin drop from my back. By the time I reached Amarillo, Texas, the itching had stopped, flaking was subsiding, and after a good wash in the shower, I could tell that the skin was healing. I gave it one more application of tincture that night in Amarillo, and by the time I arrived back in California in two days, the skin on my back was perfectly normal. Seven days across the country with five days of iodine treatment and my skin was again in good health.

All during this trip I was trying to figure out what could have caused the itching rash on my back. When I took that last swim, the water was quite warm and I knew that the dinoflagellates were blossoming and thought that it may have been these tiny toxic little organisms, but then, the rash should be all over my body and not limited to my back, and the same should apply for any other little organism that might find its way into my skin. I didn't think that I had been in contact with poison ivy or oak, besides, my back should have been covered and this itchy rash was not like the poison oak rashes that I would get once in a while on the ranch in Atascadero, CA. Then I thought that a jelly fish may have brushed against my back without any notice, or even just the tentacles could have brushed unnoticeably against my back, and this was the time of year for jelly fish reproduction. This would be the reason for the limitation of the itching to my back, but I thought that jelly fish nettles acted immediately and stung immediately. I reasoned that some species of jelly fish nettle cells might not blast of immediately, took a little time for the release of the nettles, or time for the nettles to work their way into the skin, possibly with a little help, or pressure from an outside object such as a shirt or a body while laying on a bed. That would account for the delay in the action of the nettle toxin. The toxin in the nettle cells of the species that brushed against my back may not have been very toxic, which only brought a mild rash with sloughing of the cornified layer and itching sensation to the skin of humans. I settled on thoughts that the skin problem on my back was the result of nettles from jelly fish. If not, it may have been something more serious that rapid application and continued treatment with tincture of iodine rapidly and totally eliminated.

A MISPLACED REGENERATING NERVE

I have encountered another instance in which treatment with iodine has overcome an unusual skin problem. About seven years ago I noticed a small area about two millimeters in diameter and five millimeters down from the outer edge of the fingernail on my left middle finger, the one next to my index finger.

My studies told me that this little cornified growth near the tip of my middle finger was the result of a nerve that had been cut. The nerve ending regenerated but did not find or reinervate its original target. This type of nerve ending can wander around in the tissues for years trying to find the molecular configuration that is complementary to the molecular configuration at the tip of the nerve ending. If it doesn't find a match, the tip of the nerve sometimes ends up in the papillary layer of the epidermis. In this position the nerve ending stimulates a few papillary cells to divide faster than usual. As they cornify in larger quantity than the surrounding epithelial cells they push the surrounding cells out and form a little pocket or pit of cornified cells like the little pit near the tip and to the outer side of my finger.

I attempted to see if tincture of iodine might stop the growth of this little pit that was filled with a sphere of cornified epithelial cells. I probed this little area with a pair of very sharply pointed watchmakers forceps and found that I could remove the hard cornified cells as one tightly packed little elongate lump. This left a pit about two millimeters in diameter. The first time that I did this I simply left the empty pit without any further treatment. About two months later that little pit had filled in with cornified cells again. I removed the cornified cells and this time I filled in the pit with tincture of iodine and filled it again for the next two days and forgot about it. Six months later I noticed that the little pit had again attained a diameter of a noticeable two millimeters and was again filled with a sphere of cornified cells. I removed the sphere once again and picked out a deeper layer of cornified cells. Now the bottom of the pit was a pink color so I had probed a little deeper this time. I filled the pit and surrounding area with tincture of iodine and let it dry, and repeated this two more times, now it was an almost black color. For the next three days I repeated this routine and then stopped. The little pit disappeared in about a week and I didn't see any new growth for at least six months when I noticed the appearance of a cornified pit in the same spot as before but this time it was only one millimeter in diameter. A few weeks passed and then I removed the cornified cells with sharp watchmakers forceps and removed a layer of cornified tissue around the pit, and went into the bottom of the pit to remove little bits of tissue until it looked red but wasn't bleeding. I was determined to eliminate that unusual growth of cornified cells. Once again I gave it the iodine treatment for six days in a row, let it go without treatment for a few days, removed the cornified tissue in the treated area, and gave it three more treatments over three days. Not long ago more than two years passed without a sign of that little pit of cornified cells, and I said to myself, maybe I finally eliminated the effects of that lost broken nerve. Then, a few days ago, I thought that I felt a little hard spot to the side of my fingernail, the spot with the pit of cornified cells. I took a closer look and sure enough, there it was a sphere of cornified cells about a millimeter across, but it didn't seem as deep as before. That little pit was absent for over two years but it looks like it's time for another treatment.

SMALL AREAS OF ABNORMAL EPITHELIAL GROWTH

One last abnormal epithelial growth that I have treated with tincture of iodine. About four years ago I noticed an area toward the back of my arm about ten inches down from the top of my shoulder. This area was a little over a centimeter in diameter with small (1 to 3 millimeters) irregular reddened areas scattered about. Some of the little reddened areas had bits of cornified epithelium projecting from their surface. I didn't know what was going on within this small area but I didn't like the looks of it and thought that it might be precancerous. I brought out my little brown bottle of iodine and gave that area its first treatment. Unfortunately this area didn't get sore or itch so it was easy to forget. I didn't give it another soaking with iodine for a week, and at that time the entire area was rough with sloughing cornified cells. I tried to be more consistent with the treatments, and sometimes I would treat the area with tincture every day for a week. It would lose the reddened spots, stop sloughing the cornified layer, and except for a little roughness, take on the appearance of the skin around it. I would forget it for a couple of months and when I looked at it again, it was back to its original appearance. I would treat it for two or three days and forget it again, but with these brief treatments it would never disappear but it never did get larger.

I maintained this inconsistent pattern for over two years and then about two years ago, another area with the same pattern and size appeared on the skin of my abdomen about five inches below my left nipple. This frightened me a bit so I started iodine treatment immediately. This abnormal area was right at my front so I would see it every day with a reminder to apply iodine. Once a day every day I gave it an application of iodine, at the same time I treated the area on the back of my right arm. At first the area on my abdomen was very rough and would slough many cornified cells every day. After about a month, sloughing cornified cells began to subside, I continued treatment every day and after another month, sloughing was confined to a few slightly reddened areas. I applied tincture of iodine to this area for another month and by this time I could no longer tell the former abnormal area from the surrounding skin, and stopped treating this area. In the year and a half since, there is absolutely no indication that the abnormal cornification will return. It is now impossible to locate the former location of this abnormal skin rash.

After a month of treating the area on my abdomen, another area with the same characteristics appeared near the back of my left leg toward the inner side, and about six inches from my knee. This area was larger, about a centimeter and a half across, very actively sloughing cornified cells, and became itchy every now and then. After I detected this area, I immediately began iodine application. Now I was applying iodine to three small areas of my body. Even after treatment for a month, the area on my leg was still actively sloughing cornified cells. I tried scratching the cornified area and picking excess tissue away and then applying iodine.

This burned a little but stopped the itching and that felt good. Sometimes I would give this area two treatments in a day. During the next month the itching stopped and the cornification declined rapidly so that I could hardly tell where to apply the iodine, but I continued to apply iodine to the area for another month. This lesion on my leg was eliminated over a year and a half ago and shows no sign of returning.

All the while I continued treatment to the one centimeter area on the back of my arm. After the affected areas on my abdomen and leg appeared to be cured, two to three to four little red spots with associated cornified cells continued to appear within the original one centimeter area on the back of my arm. This area was more persistent, but I didn't vigorously attack this area with iodine for at least two years after its first detection. Now I was treating it with tincture in the morning and at night until it turned a very deep brown. After about a month of this treatment, the littlest red spots gradually disappeared but I continued to treat the area for another month and stopped. A year passed and the area on the back of my arm appeared to be cured but I inspected this area a week ago and saw three little irregular spots right in the original one centimeter, so I started iodine applications once again.

Rapid and vigorous treatment with iodine is far better and much more effective than letting these abnormal growths continue to survive for a longer period of time. With time they apparently establish deeper or even latent roots that permit renewed growth after iodine treatment has ceased.

IODINE ACTS ON ABNORMAL CELLS

Iodine appears to act on cells that have an abnormality such as a virus, or whatever caused that totally excessive cornification and itching on my back after that swim in Buzzards Bay, or with those possibly precancerous growths on my arm, abdomen, and leg. I went without a hat for most of my life and now have areas on the top of my head that have excessive cornification and some of these are more than likely precancerous. I treat these with iodine and that keeps them under control without having an effect on cells without excessive cornification. To see what would happen I have placed inch long strips of iodine on the cheeks of my face and applied iodine over the same strips the following day. Within five to seven days, I could peel a very thin one inch strip of cornified epithelium from the place I applied the iodine. That was the only effect. In this case I don't think that the iodine penetrated beyond the layer of cornified cells. This kind of action gives me the impression that iodine is not absorbed by normal skin cells, hence, does not act on normal cells only on abnormal cells.

Two final notes on the use of iodine for the treatment of skin ailments. The brown metallic tincture version must be used. The colorless variety does not work. On my body, the treatment of my skin with tincture of iodine has never left a scar, the surface of my skin has always become as normal as the surrounding skin.

Chapter 11

A FORMULA FOR GETTING A^s IN CLASSES

THE SIGNIFICANCE OF MAGICAL NUMBERS

When I was an undergraduate I didn't begin to think about the magical numbers 15 and 120, let alone their origin, or their significance? At first they were numbers that I had to endure for fulfillment of requirements, but one finds the importance of these numbers when registering for classes or applying for graduation. Another puzzlement was about how to study, an important item for which I received no instruction in high school, as an undergraduate or graduate student. We were always left to fumble through the best we could. In this chapter I offer my support in these matters.

The university/college class system is setup for 15 units per semester, two semesters a year gives 30 units per year and 120 units for four years, the required number for graduation. Fifteen units at 3 units per class requires five classes per semester. Each 3 unit lecture class meets the equivalent of three times a week for 50 minutes plus 10 minutes for time to move from one class to the next, or one hour per unit, or three hours a week for each class. Classes with laboratories require 3 hours of time for each unit. With most lab classes meeting 2 times a week, an additional 4 hours of time would have to be added to the weekly time allotment for every 2 units of lab, but I shall limit this discussion to classes without labs. Fifteen units would require fifteen hours, or 3 units per class at 5 classes per week would bring the same fifteen hours in class per week.

THE 45 HOUR SCHOOL WEEK

For a C in a class the standard requirement is 2 hours of outside work for every hour spent in class so for 15 hours in class that would be 30 hours outside of class for a guaranteed C, plus the 15 hours in class. That would make 45 hours per week for 5 classes. This amounts to a little more than a standard 40 hour work week and would be the basis for establishing 15 units of classes per semester as the standard. For a B in a class the standard is 3 hours of outside work for every hour spent in class, that would be 45 hours of work outside of class plus 15 hours in class or a 60 hour work week. That isn't so bad for a B. For an A the standard would be placed at 4 hours of outside work for every hour in class, or 60 hours per week, plus 15 hours in class or 75 hours per week. This seems excessive for As in classes but this is for all classes. Besides, seventy-five hours for an A isn't all that bad. For a 24 hour day at 7 days a week, that would be 3 hours for time in class for each of 5 days, 8.6 hours of study outside of class, 8 hours for sleep, and 4.4 hours for whatever might be desired. On a daily basis for a 5 day week for an A, that would average 3 hours a day for 3 classes, and 12 hours a day for study outside of class, plus 8 hours for sleep, and one hour for what else might be required. The 5 day week is not very reasonable.

I think that almost everyone admitted to a university/college could get As if they put in 75 hours of outside work per week. However, I have found that I can get As on the 60 hour work week schedule, so the amount of time required for individuals to achieve a goal of As in all classes will certainly vary with the individual. The standards apply to all students who are admitted to university/college and guarantee a grade that all individuals can attain if they devote that amount of time to a particular class or to all classes.

THE IDEAL CLASS SCHEDULE

For scheduling classes, the ideal is to schedule classes so that you have an hour after each class. Right after the class ends take that hour to go over the material that was covered in class. This review sets the material into perspective in short term memory and prepares it for long term memory. At this time don't go to the reading assignments, save that for later, only go through the material covered in class. Most of the time this study session will help set/place most items in establishing new neural paths that can later be recalled in a flash. The path began during class so this will reinforce the establishment of that path for future reference.

WRITTEN LISTS OF KEY WORDS

Make a written list of the items that were mentioned in class. Writing is important because it involves movement of muscles, touch, feel, and pressure with the fingers; it involves coordination between the eyes and the motion and touch of the fingers; while the brain supplies information for spelling by providing the correct letters in sequence, by providing almost microscopic movement of the fingers to form the letters and processes the new information at the same time. I found it convenient to make the lists on a folded half sheet of paper or on three by five cards. Write the list on the face of the folded sheet and hints or clues on the folded side or on the back of the cards. I found the sheets more convenient, I could get quite a few words on one sheet and they were far less bulky than the cards and easier to store in order. When you unfold the sheet the hints will be there to match the words. By all means save the sheets and cards they will be used later. During the hour after class the material from the class will still be fresh in mind and you might be surprised how it comes back right from its presentation in class and this further establishes a neural path to this information.

If the ideal of a free hour after each class cannot be attained, go for two classes in a row with a two hour break after the second class. Then go over the material and make lists for the first class first and then the second class, but do not put it off, the neural paths will begin to fade and reinforcement will become more difficult and more laborious.

USING THE LISTS

That evening bring out the list and go over each item mentally, this takes much less time than writing it out, so you can go through the list reasonably rapidly if you have explanations for most items. Describe it, tell what it does, define it, give an argument for or against, give its location, whatever is needed to give it meaning for the class. If you can say something about each item, that will finish that list for the day. Now on another sheet of paper see if you can write down every item on the list without looking at the original list. Each time you write down an item on the list, a mental picture of the meaning of that item will come to the forefront and the neural path to that item will be reinforced. If you leave out some of the items, start a new permanent sheet with those items on it, review the meaning of those items again, and then write down those items to see if you can recall every item on that short list. I think that you will be surprised at how much you can recall after only hearing it in class, writing it after class, and reviewing it once that evening.

The first time you go through the list explanations may not come so readily, then I find that scribbling (it doesn't have to be neat, you are doing it only for yourself) what I know on paper often brings out the explanation for an item. If you have to look it up write that on the list on the folded side of your list. If you get stuck again a few choice words written on the folded side will remind you what you had to look up.

LISTS FROM READING MATERIAL

If reading material has been assigned, preferably, read the material before class that will help you understand the material as it was being presented in class, but if you do not find time to do the reading before class, do it after class. In my classes I very rarely read the material before class, I would read it after class. Nevertheless, while going through the reading, make a separate list of items that are important for the class. I would almost always use required books as reference books. I tried to take very good notes and succeeded most of the time, so if I didn't understand something from class notes, I would go to the required books and make a list of things that didn't appear on my list from lecture. Most of the time the list that I made from lecture would cover the required items, and sometimes I wouldn't understand the material after looking it up in the book. Then what would I do? Go to the library and look it up in an entirely different source or sources. As a matter of fact, after you have gone over the lists and can give an explanation for every item without hesitation, then you know the material, so if you have time go to the library and read about it from a different source. In science classes, I found it extremely interesting to go to an original source such as a journal from which the material was obtained.

Some classes have assigned reading that is not covered in class. In this instance, making lists on the reading material can be very helpful, but you must keep in mind that the list should be in reference to topics that the instructor thinks you should know about even though they are not covered in class. In other words, the lists should be directed toward the class and how the material relates to the class, don't' write down every little thing that comes along, figure out how it relates to class and write words that will refresh the memory of those thoughts.

LISTS FORM THE BASIS OF MY STUDY SCHEME

Now that I have lists, how do I make use of them? Let us say that I made my first list after the first day of class. I have gone over this list two times and have given useful explanations for everything but ten items. I have looked up these ten items and placed choice words opposite these items on the folded side of the sheet for the list. Then I tried to recall all the words on the list by writing them in list fashion on another sheet of paper. I succeeded in recalling all but five of the items on the list and stopped at this point. Two days later I had this class again and made the second list for this class. I repeated exactly what I did for the first list and stopped. Then I took up the first list and attempted to give mental explanations for all the items on the first list. This went fairly rapidly for the items that I knew, but I had difficulty with twelve items. I had difficulty with seven of these items the first time and had to look at the choice words to recall the explanations that I had given for these items. Then I went over this list again and briefly visualized the items that I knew, and concentrated on the items I missed and found it helpful to write brief shorthand type explanations for these words. Then I tried to recall all the words on this list by writing them in list fashion on a new sheet of paper and usually succeeded in remembering all the words and stopped at that point. When the weekend came along I would go over the most recent lists for all courses and give mental explanations for all items on the lists. After the weekend a new class would come and I would make out a new list for that class and go over this list exactly as I did for the first list, but this would be the third list for the class. After finishing with the third list I would go through the first list and the second list and give mental explanations for all the items on those lists and recall all the words on those lists by writing the words for those lists on a separate sheet of paper as a test. Just as I did with the first list after I finished writing the recall test for the second list. By this time the words on the first list should be in memory, so I would no longer go over this list every time I made a new list for the class but would go over the first list only once a week. Time to make a list for the fourth class. After testing for recall of the words on the list for the fourth class, I would go over the words for the second and third classes and test myself for the words in the lists for these classes. By now the words for the second class should be in memory and this list would be relegated to the weekly review.

Now we can see how the scheme would continue. Three lists would come under close scrutiny after making a new list for a new class or for new reading material. The third oldest list in the group would then be placed into the group that is reviewed on a weekly basis, and the new list for the new class would be brought in to replace the oldest list, so only three lists would be active after each class period. The weekly review of lists would build each week and become more familiar with each passing week with the oldest becoming so familiar that they should take very little time, but they should be reviewed to maintain quick and easy pathways through the brain and settlement into longer term memory.

THE BRAIN THRIVES ON CHANGE AND NEW INFORMATION

When I was an undergraduate I often thought that my brain was becoming over stuffed with information, it feels like it might burst at any moment. Perhaps if I give it too much material it will start to replace old information with new and I will lose all the old information. That would be a disaster. Fortunately, the brain doesn't work that way, the brain never gets overstuffed and never replaces old information with the new. My brain thrives on new information and actively seeks new situations and new material with which to become familiar, and I believe that all human brains function in this manner. If I walk passed a blank wall or a bulletin board with only a few items on it on one day and go by the same wall and bulletin board the next day and find a notice taped to the wall and a new notice on the bulletin board, I will stop and read those notices because the eye catches them immediately and my brain tells me that we have new information here, take note, it could be important. However, if I pass that same wall and bulletin board the next day or the next week, I will pay little attention to either notice and my brain will automatically tell me that it already knows what those notices mean, no need to look at them again. In another situation, if I walk or drive the same path every day all the details along that path become so familiar that I pay no attention to all the details, but if a flower blooms along that path, or if a dead rat or a new bird appears along the way, or if a house gets painted a different color, or a new sign appears, the eye immediately catches those changes, the brain takes over and absorbs the new information while paying absolutely no attention to the other already familiar surroundings. The brain constantly seeks new information, thrives on that information, and can never be overstuffed.

GRADUATE SCHOOL WAS VERY DIFFERENT

Did I develop this scheme for my studies as an undergraduate at U.C., Berkeley? No, but I wish that I had something like the scheme outlined above as a form of initial guidance. Nor did I develop a plan for studies as a graduate student at U.C., Los Angeles, but graduate studies are a little different and the motivation is different. For formal courses with textbooks, I would take no more than one a semester, I would take good notes, study the notes, look things up in the book, and read a different source in the library or look up the original literature, these were science courses so the tests were usually always from lecture material. It would have been very helpful to have review lists from some of the courses that I took as an undergraduate. These lists and new lists from courses in graduate school could have been very useful, especially for review for big exams like the comprehensive written and oral exams for advancement to candidacy for a doctorate.

MOTIVATION FOR GRADUATE SCHOOL

Most graduate classes involved the original literature and many oral presentations and discussions, and material from the most recent scientific journals. The motivation for graduate school classes was very different. As an undergraduate at Berkeley, the only real motivation that I had was myself. I did have some very notable professors, and with two exceptions, they were only slightly motivational from a distance, I only saw them in large lecture halls. I know that professors can motivate their students because many of my undergraduate and graduate students were highly motivated to do the best that they could. I know that they were striving to show me that they could understand the material in my courses because most worked very hard to get no less than Bs on the rather straight forward but comprehensive exams that I would give. The man with whom I did my doctoral work was a true wonder, and he and his graduate students were very motivational.

I BECAME A STUDENT AGAIN

I worked out my study scheme with lists of key words after I retired from teaching and research, and once again became a student when I returned to university, San Jose State University, and entered the states Over Sixty Program. When I was sixty-five I decided to see if I still had the brain power to make the President's Scholars List, meaning president of the university. That meant As in 15 units of classes for two semesters in the same university year. If I didn't make the Presidents List, perhaps I could make the Dean's Scholars List with a grade point average of 3.5. I developed my study scheme over the two years prior to my attempt to make the Presidents List and was getting As in all my classes but I was only taking 6 to 9 units and this would be a real test of the scheme.

TESTING THE POWER OF MY BRAIN

For the second time around, I wanted to take classes that I missed while I was becoming a scientist, so I was taking classes in art, anthropology, archeology, and auditing physics courses. I decided that four rather rigorous art history courses and a research project would sufficiently test the power of my brain. The first semester I arranged my schedule to have two art history classes on two days with an hour between classes, and two more art history classes on another two days with one class right after the other. The fifth class was my research project with ceramics. There was an ancient Etruscan account of a large ceramic sculpture that became larger rather than smaller after it was fired. I wanted to see if it was possible to make a ceramic that expanded in volume after it was fired, and if so, determine what made it possible.

After my first class, I went over my lecture notes and looked up pictures of the paintings and sculptures that we were supposed to know. I made lists of pertinent words that needed definition or that would remind me of a point that was made in class, or a word that would remind me of historically important aspects of the art work under consideration. These classes were an hour and a half long, so I had to move along in order to finish before the next class. After the next class I went to the library or Student Union to make out the list for that class. Then I went over the list for the first class and to my surprise I had an explanation for almost everything. Going over the class material immediately after class was a very good thing to do, the points made in class were vividly fresh and readily visualized in my mind and it definitely reinforced the neural path that had been established. Then I tried to make out the test list for the first class. I found it rather natural to start at the top with the first word and proceed to the last word. After writing the first word, which was always the easiest, the other words would follow and that would be in sequential order as they were presented in class, so that gave an indication of where I was in the class presentation. If I didn't get them quite right the first time, I would do the list again and the words would fall into proper order. Then I went over the list for the second class, and didn't do as well as I did for the first class so I went through that list again, and then tested my command of the words on the list for the second class by writing the list on a new piece of paper, and stopped for the day. Later that evening, I looked at the pictures of the pieces of art that were presented in class and pointed out pertinent aspects.

I reserved Friday for research but I would carry on at other times too, particularly, in the evenings several times a week.

MY STUDY SCHEME WORKED WELL

I found that my study scheme worked exceedingly well. I didn't have to study or cram for exams, I knew the material and how to use it. I followed my plan through two semesters and found the most important item was going over my notes and making lists as soon as possible after class. If I put it off for even one day, it became much more difficult to make the list and give explanations for the items on the list. The material from class did not come through as vividly as it did when I went over my notes and made out the lists in the hour or two that followed the class, so that was important in strengthening the neural pathway to the new information. It was an interesting experience not to cram for exams like I did when I was an undergraduate at Berkeley.

I MADE THE PRESIDENT'S SCHOLARS LIST

Using my study scheme made it easy to get As in all five classes over two semesters. I made the President's Scholars List and for that I was asked to join the national scholar fraternity, Phi Kappa Phi, which I did, received a fraternity pin, a medallion commemorating the event, and was asked to write a brief statement about myself for inclusion in the Who's Who for that year. As for research, I produced a ceramic that expanded in volume after it was fired. As a mater of fact I carried this finding to an extreme and made a number of ceramic pieces that floated on water. The work on volume increase was quantitative and was presented at a meeting of the American Institute of Archeology. The volume increase that I was able to demonstrate validated the possibility that the Etruscan story was true. The ceramic statue in the story could very well have increased in size after it was fired. This work was published in an A.I.A. volume that described the meeting.

Developing and putting my study scheme to work after the age of sixty-five proved to be very self-rewarding, perhaps, other students could benefit from such a scheme.